Le —
Thanks for your
help to make
this book
possible —
Richard

Spiritual Gems from
The Imitation of Christ

THE FOLLOWING OF CHRIST—"Anyone who wishes to follow Me must deny himself, take up his cross, and follow Me" (Mk 8:34).

Spiritual Gems
from
The Imitation of Christ

Compiled and edited by
RICHARD DAVIS

CATHOLIC BOOK PUBLISHING CORP.
NEW JERSEY

NIHIL OBSTAT: Fr. Philip-Michael F. Tangorra, S.T.L.
Censor Librorum

IMPRIMATUR: ✚ Most Rev. Arthur J. Serratelli, S.T.D., S.S.L., D.D.
Bishop of Paterson
August 28, 2015

Excerpts from *The Imitation of Christ* are taken from *The Imitation of Christ* by Thomas à Kempis and edited by Clare L. Fitzpatrick, copyright © 1993, 1988, 1977 by Catholic Book Publishing, Corp., Totowa, NJ, www.catholicbookpublishing.com. Used by permission. All rights reserved.

(T-342)
ISBN 978-1-941243-39-8
© 2015 Catholic Book Publishing Corp., NJ

Printed in China
www.catholicbookpublishing.com

FOREWORD

The Imitation of Christ has become one of the most powerful Christian devotional books ever written. It has influenced millions of people across the globe through its many editions and translations over hundreds of years. Though apparently intended for an audience of German monks, its influence among those who are Christian has transcended sectarian lines. It has influenced prominent religious figures such as John Wesley, founder of Methodism; Sir Thomas More, author of *Utopia*; and John Henry Newton, an Anglican clergyman and author of "Amazing Grace."

The reach of the book is undisputed, but its origins are murkier. It appears to have been written sometime early in the 15th century. According to the *Catholic Encyclopedia*, it was published in 1418. There is no certainty about who penned the manuscript, but most scholars agree on the identity of the author. The anonymity of the author certainly corresponds to the tone of the book regarding humility rather than pride. Without a person to pay attention to, the focus is on the work itself. Undoubtedly, that would please the author.

Most ascribe the manuscript to a monk named Thomas Haemmerlein or Thomas à Kempis. There are several evidences of his authorship: one is the fact that his style of writing from other works is similar to the writing in this book. Second, several of his contemporaries (including members of his monastic order) attributed the work to him. Finally, some manuscripts of around that time period identify him as the author.

Thomas was not a cosmopolitan who travelled the world. Instead, he lived a quiet life copying manuscripts and reading. He spent seventy years of his life in a monastery near Zwolle, a town currently in the Netherlands. Many of those years he spent as the subprior of his monastery.

Those unfamiliar with *The Imitation of Christ* might wonder what a 15th century monk would have to say that might be relevant to 21st century Christians. The question is valid. The times in which Thomas à Kempis lived were far different than today. Then, there was no Internet or mass media at all. People did not commute to work stuck in cars on clogged freeways. No one watched a movie or a television show. News traveled slowly, even across short distances. There were no microwaves, smart phones, space shuttles, or atomic bombs.

Religion was different as well. Relatively few people read the Bible. The Roman Catholic Church dominated the Western world since the Protestant Reformation had not yet occurred. Christian churches common today—Lutherans, Baptists, Methodists, Episcopalians, Presbyterians, Mormons, Seventh-day Adventists, etc.—did not yet exist.

Moreover, Thomas à Kempis' own life was very different from the lifestyles of people today, including the vast majority of Christians. His life was quiet and contemplative. It was devoid of other cares beyond the monastery. As a priest, he never married or had a family. He never held a job outside the monastery from the time he entered the cloister at the age of 16.

Yet, there are weighty truths located within its pages that have a timeless quality. Thomas wrote of faith, prayer, humility, and many other topics that are just as relevant today as they were six hundred years ago. He frequently quoted Scripture and occasionally spoke esoterically, but he also offered practical advice on how to live as a follower of Christ.

Yet, despite his cloistered life, Thomas was not unfamiliar with the struggles of discipleship. Indeed, this book suggests he was well acquainted with challenges to spirituality that are common to people who seek to follow Christ today, regardless of their religious affiliation. In this book, he discussed temptation, pride, and adversity—all of which he must have endured. He faced his own set of challenges in living as God wished him to. The principles he expressed can apply to our own set of challenges in doing the same today.

The author of the text clearly was Catholic. But *The Imitation of Christ* is not just for Catholics. It contains spiritual gems that can be applicable to all Christians. These include sections and verses concerning the nature of man, grace, gratitude, purity, and many other topics he addressed throughout *The Imitation of Christ.*

There is a strong asceticism in *The Imitation of Christ.* This has led to criticism of the author as being too austere for the modern age. It is true that Thomas does advocate denial of physical things. He talks about being "separated from all earthly things" and rejecting "outward comfort" or "human comfort." He also calls worldly delights "empty or unclean." To him "food, drink, and clothing, and all the other needs appertaining to the support of the body, are burdensome to the devout spirit."

Yet, the principle of putting God first and physical lusts and desires after is one that can be applicable to all. Jesus said that devils could not come out without fasting and prayer (Mark 9:29). And Jesus himself fasted frequently to draw closer to the Father.

However, Christians are not required to eschew the physical and have complete distaste for it. Indeed, Thomas does include a prayer that he "may use such things with moderation, and that I be not entangled with inordinate affection for them." And he admits that to "cast away all these things is not lawful, because nature must be sustained."

Thomas also speaks frequently of withdrawing and not associating with others. That may be more relevant to some in a monastic order, but not to most people. Indeed, such an aloofness from sociality would be difficult for the vast majority of people. Nor would it even be wise. If one has family, work, and other social obligations, pulling away from social contact would be considered a derogation of duty. Most people have responsibilities towards parents, spouse, children, work associates, friends, and neighbors that cannot be ignored.

However, the general principle of taking time to be alone and contemplate is just as relevant today as in the past. Indeed, it is more of a necessity today than in the 15th century. Too many today rush to and fro. From the moment one is awake, demands of media—cellphones, social media, television, etc. —can bombard the spirit. Indeed, it is easy to fail to take time to consider spiritual things. One of the topics discussed in this book is meditation—the need to ponder, pray, and take stock of one's life and relationship with God. That is an essential part of the Christian's life, even today.

Thomas also speaks about despising yourself. Again, that type of language may seem foreign to those of us today who seek to find the good in ourselves and others. The use of the term "despise" sounds harsh to us, but I believe it is his attempt to avoid the sin of pride. We can despise those aspects of our behavior and attitudes that are sinful while still recognizing the love that we give others and the good that we do. Nevertheless, we must remember not to place our good qualities out of perspective to the point that we become proud of them and therefore proudful.

It may be easy to dismiss the work of a 15th century monk as irrelevant. But an open-minded reader of _The Imitation of Christ_ cannot help but conclude that Thomas à Kempis held profound thoughts about relationships, temptations, and life in general that are applicable in our day. Indeed, there are many passages in _The Imitation of Christ_ that can be useful to Christians everywhere, as well as to those who are not Christians. There are messages of hope and peace and faith that resonate across cultural and religious divides. Thomas' emphasis on humility, love of others, and simplicity have universal application to all humans.

But the strongest message of _The Imitation of Christ_ is, as its title suggests, a love of, and discipleship toward, Jesus Christ. Thomas' love of the Savior is evident throughout his book. He is remarkably perceptive about the attitudes a disciple of Christ should hold, as well as the behavior necessary for following Christ. Christ is the center of his work and the effort to emulate Christ the objective of his life.

However, *The Imitation of Christ* is a difficult read for many modern readers. One reason is its nature as a compilation of sayings rather than a complete book. Reportedly, it was drawn from various sermons for monastic novices. It is organized around four books that overlap in subject matter, but appear to have been written separately from one another. It is not organized topically, which would allow the reader easily to turn to specific sections relevant to a particular theme.

As a result, the modern reader may miss the thematic threads within the book. It would be a shame if those who might benefit most from the messages Thomas à Kempis sought to convey are put off by an unfamiliar organization and writing style. This book you are reading now is intended to rectify that situation. My hope is that it will make the task of finding spiritually-uplifting passages from *The Imitation of Christ* on a particular theme easier for the typical reader.

The purpose of this book is to glean those spiritual gems in a thematic manner. By organizing passages from *The Imitation of Christ* by topic, the modern reader will be able to see the thematic connections among the four books. This topical approach also provides the reader with the ability to pick and choose which theme to read about at any given time.

For example, if the reader currently is experiencing severe trials in his or her life, the section on adversity could be most useful. Or if the reader wants to learn more about grace, humility, or charity, the passages related to those subjects can be explored. The reader can refer back to that section containing passages that will be most relevant as new challenges arise in life. Hopefully this is a book that will be referred to again and again.

It is essential to say what this book is not. This is not an exhaustive listing of all the passages in *The Imitation of Christ*; in other words, this is not the whole book in another form. Rather, it is a large sample of the passages of the book relevant to these topics.

Nor is it a commentary on the book. With the exception of brief introductions to the topical sections and the individual passages, these words come from *The Imitation of Christ*. My intent is to allow Thomas à Kempis to speak largely for himself.

I hope the reader of this book, who also has read *The Imitation of Christ*, gains a greater appreciation for Thomas à Kempis' efforts to define a path to Christ for the believer. For those who have never read it, I hope it offers further understanding of what is contained in *The Imitation of Christ*. But the most important goal to me is that when the reader, whoever he or she is, places this book down, it is with a greater determination to imitate Christ.

CONTENTS

Chapter *Page*

THE WISDOM OF JESUS—His parents found Jesus in the temple "sitting among the teachers, listening to them and asking them questions. And all who heard Him were amazed at His intelligence and His answers" (Lk 2:46f).

CHAPTER 1

Adversity

Thomas à Kempis lived most of his life quietly in a monastery. One might conclude that, with his monastic lifestyle, he was not beset with troubles. Yet, he possessed a remarkable understanding of the importance of adversity in the life of the Christian. He wrote on why we have trials, how we should not seek to avoid adversity, how God is with us in times of tribulation, and what happens to us if we endure adversity well.

Adversity will come in our lives. We should not expect that God will spare us. Indeed, such trials are good for us if we endure them well.

I thank You, O heavenly Father, that You have not spared my sins, that Your rod of correction has taught me by inflicting pains and by sending afflictions both within and without. You are the heavenly Physician, Who alone can comfort me, Who—in the midst of wounds—heals, *Who casts down to the depths of the netherworld and brings up from the great abyss* (Tob 13:2). Your tender care is upon me, and your very rod shall instruct me. (Book 3, Chapter 50)

Prepare yourself, then, to suffer all kinds of adversities and inconveniences in this wretched life; for you cannot avoid them no matter where you go, and they will find you no matter where you hide. So it is in life, and there is no avenue of escape but to keep yourself in patience. If you desire to be our Lord's dear friend and to share what is His, then you must drink heartily of His chalice. As for consolations, leave those to His will and He will arrange them as He sees best for you. But be you prepared to suffer tribulations and to consider them the greatest comforts, saying with St. Paul: *"I consider that the sufferings we presently endure are minuscule in comparison with the glory to be revealed in us"* (Rom 8:18), even though you alone were able to endure it all. (Book 2, Chapter 12)

Adversity that comes from rejection by others helps us avoid seeking the honors of others rather than God.

It is good that everything is not always to our liking; for adversity makes people look into their hearts in order to realize that they are exiles and must not put their hopes in any worldly thing. It is good for us to run into opposition and to have others think badly of us, even when our intentions are good. For these things help us to be humble and rid us of pride. Then we seek God more earnestly, Who alone knows our inmost self, when outwardly we are ignored and discredited by others. Therefore, people should rely so entirely on God that they have no need to look for human consolations when adversity comes. When people of good disposition are afflicted or tempted or distracted by evil thoughts, then they understand the need they have of God and that without Him they can do nothing. (Book 1, Chapter 12)

Our adversities test whether we are truly devout.

Through temptations and trials our spiritual progress is tested. If we are fervent and devout and unaware of any difficulties, it is no credit to us; but if we endure patiently in the time of temptation or adversity, then our spiritual advancement is apparent. (Book 1, Chapter 13)

We should not seek to avoid tribulation; it will come as we draw closer to God.

Christ's whole life was a cross and martyrdom; and do you expect pleasure and enjoyment for yourself? You make a grave mistake if you look for anything other than suffering; for this mortal life of ours is full of misery and surrounded with crosses. The higher persons advance in the way of perfection, the heavier will they often find crosses to be. This is because the more their love of God grows, the more painful is their exile from God. (Book 2, Chapter 12)

A time of adversity is when we are closest to being blessed by God.

When you are troubled, that is the best time for you to merit. Yes, you must pass through fire and water before you come to the place of refreshment. (Book 1, Chapter 22)

Peace can come from suffering rather than from its absence.

However, in this mortal life, our peace consists in the humble bearing of suffering and contradictions, not in being free of them, for we cannot live in this world without adversity. Those who can best suffer will enjoy the most peace, for such persons are masters of themselves, lords of the world, with Christ for their friend, and heaven as their reward. (Book 2, Chapter 3)

Adversity shows who we really are.

If everyone was perfect, what would we have to endure for the love of God? God wills us to learn to bear one another's burdens. No one is without faults, no one without a cross, no one self-sufficient and no one wise enough all alone. Therefore, we must support, comfort and assist one another, instructing and admonishing one another in all charity. Adversity is the best test of virtue. The occasions of sin do not weaken anyone; on the contrary, they show that person's true worth. (Book 1, Chapter 16)

Many are secretly self-seeking and therefore do their own will and not the will of God, though sometimes they are unaware of it. As long as things go their way, they appear to be at peace, but if they meet opposition, they become impatient and depressed. (Book 1, Chapter 14)

We must take adversity wherever it comes from and accept it gracefully as from God.

Therefore, they are not truly patient who will suffer only as much as they please and from whom they please. Persons who are really patient do not mind who causes their suffering—whether it be their superior, an equal, or someone of lower rank, or whether such a person is good and holy, or evil and unworthy. But whenever any adversity happens to them, whatever it is and from whomever it comes, or how often, they accept all gratefully as from the hand of God and consider it as a great benefit; for they well know that there is nothing we can suffer for God that goes without merit. (Book 3, Chapter 19)

Don't despair over temptation, but pray more to God for help to bear it.

We should not be discouraged when tempted, but turn in fervent prayer to God, Who, in His infinite goodness and compassion, will help us in all our needs. St. Paul has said that *"together with the trial He will also provide a way out and the strength to bear it"* (1 Cor 10:13). Let us humbly submit ourselves to God in all trials and temptations, for *it is the humble and submissive that He will save and exalt* (Ps 34:19). (Book 1, Chapter 13)

My child let not the labors which you have undertaken for My sake crush you; nor let any trouble cause you to lose heart. For whatever happens, have confidence that My promise will be your strength and consolation. I will reward you beyond all limits and measure. (Book 3, Chapter 47)

Suffering makes us more humble.

Either you will suffer bodily pain, or you will endure in your soul tribulation of spirit. Sometimes God will leave you to your own devices and sometimes your neighbor will irritate you; and what is worse, you will often be a trouble to your own self. No remedy or comfort can free you from this affliction or make it easier for you to bear; you simply have to bear your cross as long as God wills it. God wants you to learn to suffer tribulation without comfort and, submitting yourself entirely to Him, to grow in humility through tribulation. (Book 2, Chapter 12)

God is with us in our trials.

God gives consolation to make us stronger in time of adversity. (Book 2, Chapter 9)

What shall I say now, Lord, in the midst of my distress? May Your will be done, for I well deserve to be afflicted and oppressed. I must bear it—and with patience—until the storm has passed and things grow better. Your almighty hand is able to remove this temptation and to moderate its violence, as You have often done for me before, so that I do not give in to it, most merciful God! The harder this seems to me, the easier it is for You to bring about my deliverance; for this is *the change of the right hand of the Almighty* (Ps 77:11), to Whom be everlasting honor and glory. (Book 3, Chapter 29)

THE SPIRIT GUIDES US IN READING SCRIPTURE—"When [the Paraclete] the Spirit of truth comes, He will guide you into all the truth" (Jn 16:13).

JESUS OPENS OUR EYES TO FOLLOW HIM—"Jesus said to [the blind man], 'Receive your sight. Your faith has made you well.' Immediately, he received his sight and followed Jesus" (Lk 18:42f).

Our trials are only temporary.

Your labor here will not be of long duration and you shall not always be oppressed with sorrows. Wait a little while and you will see an end to all your troubles. The hour will come sooner than you think when toil and trial shall be no more; for all that passes with time is short-lived and counts but little. (Book 3, Chapter 47)

Trust in God to protect and lead in time of trial.

I labor, indeed, in the sweat of my brow; I am tormented by a sorrowful heart, burdened by my sins, troubled with temptations, and caught up in and oppressed by many evil passions, but there is no one to help me. For who can deliver me and save me, and to whom can I commit myself and all that is mine, except You, Lord God, my Savior? (Book 4, Chapter 4)

Keep yourself calm and even prepare yourself to undergo greater suffering. All is not lost just because you find yourself often in trouble and grievously tempted. Remember, you are human and not God; you are flesh and blood and not an Angel. (Book 3, Chapter 57)

Seek comfort from God and not created things, and then contentment will come.

When people reach that state where they seek consolation from no creature, then they begin to taste the sweetness of God and to be content with whatever happens. They care for no worldly profit, however great, nor pine for the want of it, because they are wholly committed to God, Who is their All—God for Whom nothing is ever lost or dies and to Whom all things live and ever obediently render service. (Book 1, Chapter 25)

> *Our current sufferings are little compared to the glory that we will experience.*

Do you believe that spiritual consolations will be yours for the asking?. . . Do you expect to have here and now what others just managed to obtain after many tears and great labors? *Place your hope in the Lord: be strong and courageous in your heart and place your hope in the Lord* (Ps 27:14). Do not despair, do not give up; but with perseverance offer both body and soul for the glory of God. Your reward will be abundant, and I will be with you in all your tribulations. (Book 3, Chapter 35)

CHAPTER 2

Charity

In 1 Corinthians 13, Paul speaks of faith, hope, and charity. Of these, he says, the greatest is charity. Thomas à Kempis also valued charity, particularly above other traits we often seek as a substitute, such as the honors of others or scriptural or secular knowledge. We are often tempted not to be charitable towards others as we bump up against each other in everyday life. These passages remind us of the necessity of charity in our daily lives, as well as the importance of our motive in our charitable works.

Charity is a higher virtue than knowledge.

Those who abound in charity are truly great. (Book 1, Chapter 3)

If your knowledge encompasses the universe and the love of God is not in you, what good will it do you in God's sight. He will judge you according to your actions. (Book 1, Chapter 2)

We will be judged not by our piety, scriptural knowledge, or status, but on our humility and charity.

The merits of persons are not to be highly esteemed because such persons have many visions or spiritual consolations, or because they are well versed in Scripture, nor even by their being in a more elevated position. But if they are firmly grounded in humility and filled with charity... in the end they will have the reward of God for all their labor. (Book 3, Chapter 7)

Charity is not doing great things, but doing what we can.

Without charity the outward deed is worthless; but whatever is done out of charity, no matter how small and insignificant, is profitable in the eyes of God, Who looks not so much at what we do, as to the love with which we do it. (Book 1, Chapter 15)

Our motives in doing charity must not be selfish, but to glorify God.

True charity is not self-seeking, but goes all the way for the honor and glory of God. Those who are charitable envy no one, nor do they seek their own pleasure, but desire above all things to find their joy in God. How well they know that no good begins in humans and so they refer all to God, from Whom all things come and in Whom all the Saints find their eternal blessedness. If they had only a spark of real charity, they would know in their souls that all earthly things are vain. (Book 1, Chapter 15)

Those who love God much do much, and those do a deed well who perform it for the common good and not to please themselves. Often what appears to be charity is really done for carnal motives—self-love, the hope of a reward or some personal advantage seldom being absent. (Book 1, Chapter 15)

Divine charity prevents vices.

If heavenly grace and true charity enter into your heart, there will be no room for envy, no narrowness of heart, nor will self-love rule in you. For the charity of God overcomes all and will expand and set on fire the powers of your soul. (Book 3, Chapter 9)

CHAPTER 3

Contrition

Contrition is sorrow for the sins we have committed. We may believe contrition is bad because it is connected with feeling guilty for what we do. Or we may be too proud to feel contrition and conclude that it is only for the weak. But Thomas à Kempis explained the connection between contrition and grace and the need for us to possess contrition in our relationship with God.

Contrition is a feeling and not just a word.

It is better to experience contrition than to be able to define it. (Book 1, Chapter 1)

We must examine ourselves with contrition and humility.

Examine your conscience carefully and, to the best of your ability, cleanse and purify it by sincere contrition and a humble confession, so that you may not be aware of anything to fill you with remorse, or prevent your free approach to God. Be sorry for all your sins in general, and especially regret and have sorrow for your daily offenses. If time permits, tell God—in the secrecy of your heart—all the miseries caused by your unruly passions. (Book 4, Chapter 7)

Contrition brings grace from God.

What else can I say but that I have sinned, Lord, I have sinned? Have mercy on me and pardon me. *Let me alone so that I may have a few moments of happiness before I go to the land of gloom and deep darkness, never again to return* (Job 10:20-21). What do You ask most, Lord, of a poor guilty sinner except repentance and self-abasement for personal sins? For true contrition and a humble heart bring forth hope of forgiveness, the troubled conscience is reconciled, and the grace that was lost is recovered and a person is secured against the wrath to come. God and the penitent soul meet together with a holy kiss. (Book 3, Chapter 52)

Humble contrition of heart is a most acceptable sacrifice to You, O Lord, which is more fragrant than burning incense. It is that sweet ointment which You welcomed to have poured over Your sacred feet; for *a contrite and humble heart, O God, You will not spurn* (Ps 51:19). There is the place of refuge from the wrath of the enemy; there whatever has been defiled is washed away. (Book 3, Chapter 52)

CHAPTER 4

Conversation

According to John Donne, "no man is an island, entire of itself; every man is a piece of the continent." Isolation is not the role of the Christian; nor is it even practical. Daily, we converse with other people. What we say to others matters. We can uplift, encourage, inspire. Or we can use our conversation to degrade and discourage through criticism or gossip. The choice is ours. In *The Imitation of*

Christ, Thomas said little about conversation, but his brief counsel about what the Christian should do in dialogue with others is useful to remember.

Avoid gossip or other vain conversation; speak things which edify.

Flee as much as possible the company of worldly people. For discussing worldly matters, no matter how good the intention, is a great obstacle to the spiritual life. If we are not careful, we can be easily deceived and attracted by the vanity of the world. Often I regret the things I have said and wished that I had not spent so much time in worldly company. We think that by getting together with others we will be a comfort to one another and find relaxation by discussing the things that burden us; but the end result of all this gossip about things we like or dislike only leaves us with a guilty conscience.

But the sad part of it is that all we say and do is for nothing; for the comfort we receive from others hinders us from receiving the comfort that comes from God. It is better to watch and pray so that we do not waste time in idleness. If you have leave to speak and it is expedient, then speak of God and of those things which will edify.

A bad use or neglect of our spiritual progress makes us careless of what we say. However, devout conversation on spiritual matters is beneficial to the soul, especially when people who are congenial in mind and spirit are drawn together in God. (Book 1, Chapter 10)

CHAPTER 5

Faith in God

Thomas not only was faithful, but he pondered the meaning of faith. To him, faith in God was not the antithesis of reason. Rather, it is reason's preface. Nor did he believe faith was devoid of action. Faith must be accompanied by the sincere life. He also understood that faith is essential in adversity. When we suffer trials, we are inclined to lose hope. But remaining faithful in the most dire of circumstances will result in God's reward. Faith will lead to knowledge, particularly about those things we do not now understand.

Leave mysteries alone; instead have faith and a sincere life.

That simplicity is truly blessed which departs from ways of dispute and follows the plain and sure path of God's commandments. Many have lost their devotion while searching into mysteries too deep for them to understand. Only faith and a good life are required of you, not a lofty intellect nor a probing into the deep mysteries of God. If you cannot understand or grasp those things which are beneath you, how can you comprehend those that are above you? Submit yourself humbly to God, and submit your senses to faith, and the light of knowledge will be given to you for your spiritual well-being, according to the measure of God. (Book 4, Chapter 18)

Have faith that consolation will come in due season.

Is anything impossible for Me? (Jer 32:27). Am I like human beings who promise something and do not live up to it? Where is your faith? Stand firm and persevere. Have courage and wait patiently; comfort will come to you when you most need it. Wait for Me, wait; and I will come soon to help you. (Book 3, Chapter 30)

Faith should precede reason.

All reason and natural inquiry must follow faith. (Book 4, Chapter 18)

Commit things not understood to God.

Go forward, therefore, in simple and unwavering faith, and approach this Sacrament with humble reverence. Whatever you are unable to understand, confidently entrust to Almighty God.(Book 4, Chapter 18)

God rewards the faithful.

God walks with the simple, makes Himself known to the humble, and gives understanding to the poor in spirit. He reveals His meaning to the clean of heart, but He hides His grace from the proud and curious. Human reason is weak and easily deceived; but true faith cannot be deceived. (Book 4, Chapter 18)

Trust in God rather than others.

No confidence is to be placed in mortal human beings, no matter how helpful they may be or how dear to us, for we are all frail. Neither should you be downcast if one day they are on your side and the next day they are against you; for humans are changeable like the wind. Therefore, put your complete trust in God and let Him be the center of your love and fear. He will answer for you and will do what He sees best for you. What are you but an alien and a pilgrim! Only if you are united to Christ will you have a rest. (Book 2, Chapter 1)

CHAPTER 6

Forgiveness

When Jesus was near death on the cross, He said: "Father, forgive them; for they know not what they do" (Lk 23:34). Those few words communicate two vital messages regarding forgiveness. One is that we must forgive others, even those who are reviling us. The other is that we, ourselves, can be forgiven of the sins we commit.

Thomas reminded Christians of both of those messages in *The Imitation of Christ*. He urged us to pray for those who hurt us. He also called on the Christian to seek forgiveness for sin and to "confess and lament" sins because God will extend His loving-kindness.

Confess and forsake sin and God will forgive according to His loving-kindness.

What else can I do about my sins but humbly confess and deplore them, ever asking for Your mercy? Please hear me, O merciful God, as I stand before You. All my sins are extremely detestable to me; by Your grace, I will never commit them again.

I am truly sorry for them and will regret them the rest of my life; and I am ready to do penance and make amends to the best of my ability. O my God, I beg You to forgive my sins, for Your holy Name's sake. Be pleased to save my soul, which You have redeemed by Your precious Blood. I commit myself to Your mercy, resigning myself with confidence into Your hands. (Book 4, Chapter 9)

Pray for forgiveness.

Lift up your eyes to God in heaven and beg His forgiveness for your sins. (Book 1, Chapter 20)

Lord, God, most just Judge (Ps 7:12), strong and patient, You know the frailty and the malice of human beings. I beseech You to be my strength and my guide, for my conscience of itself is not sufficient. You know what I do not know, and that even under reprimand I ought to humble myself and bear it meekly. For as often as I have not acted thus, in Your great mercy forgive me and give me the grace of greater endurance for the future. (Book 3, Chapter 46)

God will not remember our sins when we are forgiven.

If people do all they can, and are truly sorry for their sins, as often as they come to Me for grace and forgiveness, I am the Lord God, Who says: *Do I take any pleasure in the death of the wicked? . . . Do I not rather rejoice when they turn from their ways and live?* (Ezek 18:23). I will no longer remember their sins, but all will be forgiven them. (Book 4, Chapter 7)

CHAPTER 7

God's Will

We are on earth to do God's will, not our own. However, God does not force us to do so. Instead, He allows us to choose whether or not to follow His will or our own. Thomas appreciated the choice we have to make. That is why he wrote about why we should choose to do God's will, what happens to us when we follow God's will, how doing God's will is a manifestation of our love of God, and, finally, that our lives should be devoted to seeking God's will for us.

We must let God use us as He will rather than follow our own human judgment.

My child, permit Me to do with you what I will, for I know what is best for you. You think as a human being and judge things according to human reason; but you are often swayed by your feelings and worldly attitudes, so that you can easily be deceived and make mistakes. (Book 3, Chapter 17)

JESUS CALLS FOR RECONCILIATION BEFORE SACRIFICE—
"Therefore, when offering your gift at the altar, if you should remember that your brother has something against you, leave your gift there at the altar and first go to be reconciled with your brother" (Mt 5:23f).

PRELUDES TO THE LAST JUDGMENT—"Following that distress, the sun will be darkened, and the moon will not give forth its light, and the stars will be falling from the sky, and the heavenly powers will be shaken" (Mk 13:24f).

*Our perfection comes from offering our-
selves to God's will.*

Do not think, therefore, that you have found
true peace if you feel no grief, nor that all is well if
no one opposes you; nor that you have arrived at
perfection if everything goes the way you want it.
Do not entertain any notion that you are a privi-
leged person, particularly beloved by God, because you experience great fervor and devotion. It
is not in such things that a true lover of virtue is
known, nor does a person's spiritual perfection
and progress consist in these things.

In what, then, Lord, does it consist?

In surrendering yourself with your whole heart
to the will of God, and in not seeking yourself either in great things or small, in time or in eternity.
If you remain constant in this attitude, you will
continue to thank God whether things go well or
otherwise, weighing all things in the one equal balance of His love. And if you come to the state
that, when inward consolation is withdrawn, you
can move your heart to suffer still more, if God so
wills—not considering it an injustice for you to
suffer such great things, but acknowledging the
justice of all My decisions—and still praise My
holy Name, then you walk in the true way of peace
and may hope without doubt to see Me face to
face in everlasting joy in the kingdom of heaven.
(Book 3, Chapter 25)

*Wisdom comes from conforming to the
mind of God.*

Christ's teaching surpasses that of all the Saints.
But to find this spiritual nourishment you must

seek to have the Spirit of Christ. It is because we lack this Spirit that so often we listen to the Gospel without really hearing it. Those who fully understand Christ's words must labor to make their lives conform to His. (Book 1, Chapter 1)

They are truly learned who forsake their own will to follow the will of God. (Book 1, Chapter 3)

We should not seek the easy path, but receive and bear what things are laid upon us by God.

Religious persons put up with and accept willingly whatever they are commanded to do; but the neglectful and lukewarm are always in difficulty and have great anguish besides, for they lack interior comfort and cannot seek it outside. Undisciplined persons, who seek to be released from their duties, will always be in trouble, for nothing will ever satisfy them. (Book 1, Chapter 25)

Blessed are those who follow God's will.

I will hear what the Lord God will speak within me" (Ps 85:9), says a devout soul. Blessed is that soul who hears the Lord speaking within, and from His lips receives the words of comfort. Blessed are the ears that heed the inner whisperings of the Lord, and pay no attention to the deceitful murmurings of this world; and blessed indeed are the ears which do not listen to the loud voices from outside, but instead are attentive to Him, Who inwardly teaches the truth.

Blessed also are the eyes which are closed to things outside, but gaze intently on things within. Blessed are they who acquire virtue and labor, by spiritual and corporal works, to receive daily more and more God's inward inspirations and teachings. They also are blessed who determine to serve God alone, ridding themselves of every hindrance from the world. (Book 3, Chapter 1)

Seek to know the Lord's will.

Lord, *teach me to do Your will* (Ps 143:10) and to live worthily and humbly in Your sight. You are my wisdom and You know me as I truly am; You knew me before the world was made, and before I was born into this life. (Book 3, Chapter 3)

Give me the grace to understand Your will, and with great reverence and careful consideration remember all Your blessings, in general and in particular, so that from now on I may be able to thank You for them worthily. (Book 3, Chapter 22)

If we love God, we must be willing to do His will.

Those who are not always ready to suffer and to stand disposed to the will of their Beloved are not worthy to be called lovers; for lovers must gladly embrace all hardship and bitter things for their Beloved, and never allow themselves to turn away from Him by adversity. (Book 3, Chapter 5)

CHAPTER 8

Good Works

James asked whether it profits a man if he has faith, but does not have works (Jas 2:14). In *The Imitation of Christ*, Thomas urged the Christian to see the good works of others and do the same, but to be careful not to glory in those works.

Pray to God to continually do good works

Grant, therefore, O Lord, that Your grace always go before me and be ever at my back, keeping me intent upon good works to be done, through Jesus Christ, Your Son and my Lord. Amen. (Book 3, Chapter 55)

We should not glory in our good works, but remember that we are weaker than we think.

Do not consider yourself better than others, for you may be worse in God's sight. Do not be proud of your good works, for often what pleases us displeases God, Whose judgments differ from the judgment of humans. Whatever goodness or virtue is in you, believe that your neighbor has better qualities; in this way you will preserve humility. It will not hurt you to consider yourself worse than others, even if this is not really so; but it will hurt greatly if you prefer yourself above another, although that person might be a great sinner. A humble person is a peaceful person; but the hearts of the proud are full of envy and resentment. (Book 1, Chapter 7)

Think about your sins with great displeasure and deep sorrow in your heart, never considering yourself virtuous because of your good deeds. Rather, reflect on how great a sinner you are, subject to the many passions which envelop you. Left to yourself, you revert to nothing, soon fall, soon are overcome, soon are disturbed and easily discouraged. There is nothing for which you can take credit, but much for which you ought to despise yourself; for you are far weaker in spiritual things than you realize. (Book 3, Chapter 4)

Look for good examples and then go and do the same.

Use all occasions for your spiritual gain. If you observe good example, follow it; and if you see bad example, take care not to do the same; if you have already fallen into this fault, work to correct it quickly. As your eye observes others, be sure that you also are observed by them. What an inspiration to see religious persons devout and fervent in the love of God, courteous and self-disciplined! On the other hand, how sad to see those whose lives are disorderly and who do not practice those things to which they are called. How detrimental it is for us to neglect the purpose of our calling and to divert our minds to things that are not our concern. (Book 1, Chapter 25)

CHAPTER 9

Grace

Paul tells us that grace provides salvation and "not of yourselves" (Eph 2:8). Thomas sought to explain grace, particularly in contrast to nature, but also to help readers understand its virtues—its power in our lives—and to urge readers to keep God's grace and not destroy it. He wanted his readers to appreciate the process of obtaining grace.

His contrast of grace with our natures is particularly enlightening since we can see the starkness of the dichotomy between our own human nature and the manifestations of the grace of God in our lives. Reading those passages, we can engage in self-examination to assess how much we are still holding to nature rather than allowing ourselves to be transformed into a new person by grace. Thomas closed that comparison with the admonition: "The more nature is kept down and overcome, the more grace fills a human soul, and through new daily visitations the soul is formed more and more to the image of God" (Book 3, Chapter 54).

We must put our trust in God's grace.

In whom, then, can I hope, or in what may I place my trust, but in the great and endless mercy of God? (Book 2, Chapter 9)

The way of man is not in himself.

The resolution of devout persons depends more on the grace of God than on their own wisdom.

For human beings propose, but God disposes, *nor is the course of their life as they would have it* (Jer 10:23). (Book 1, Chapter 19)

By following outward things, we lose God's grace for us.

But as soon as you turn back to outward things, you will quickly drive away your Lord and lose His grace. (Book 2, Chapter 8)

My child, My grace is precious and will not be mingled with earthly things or worldly consolation. You must get rid of every impediment if you would have that priceless gift poured into your soul. (Book 3, Chapter 53)

We should seek God's grace to be poured down on us.

Send forth Your light and Your truth (Ps 43:3) to shine upon the earth; for I am like the barren and dry earth until You enlighten me. Pour forth Your grace from above and water my heart with Your heavenly dew; let streams of devotion water the face of the earth; that it may bring forth good and perfect fruit. Lift up my mind so oppressed by the burden of sin and raise up my desire to heavenly things, so that having tasted the sweetness of supernatural joy, I may have no pleasure in the thought of earthly things. (Book 3, Chapter 23)

Through grace, we are pardoned and received by God.

Wipe clean from the slate of my conscience every stain of sin and every fault; and restore to me Your grace, which I have lost through sin, granting me full pardon of all, and in Your mercy receiving me with the kiss of peace. (Book 4, Chapter 9)

God's grace empowers us.

When God's grace comes to any persons, they are made strong to do all things. (Book 2, Chapter 8)

We must be humble and grateful to receive God's grace.

However, if you attribute anything good to yourself, you only impede God's grace; for the grace of the Holy Spirit ever seeks a humble heart. (Book 3, Chapter 42)

What do You ask most, Lord, of a poor guilty sinner except repentance and self-abasement for personal sins? For true contrition and a humble heart bring forth hope of forgiveness, the troubled conscience is reconciled, and the grace that was lost is recovered and a person is secured against the wrath to come. God and the penitent soul meet together with a holy kiss. (Book 3, Chapter 52)

God does well in sending the grace of comfort, but human beings do ill in not returning all to God with thanks. Therefore, these gifts of grace cannot flow in us because of our ingratitude to the

Giver in not returning all to Him, the Source. Grace is always given to the person who is grateful, and God readily gives to the humble what is taken from the proud. (Book 2, Chapter 10)

Grace lifts our soul.

A great grace is needed to elevate the soul and lift it above itself. And unless we are so elevated and detached from creatures and completely united to God, our knowledge and our possessions are of little importance. (Book 3, Chapter 31)

Your grace is the teacher of truth, the master of discipline; it brings light to the heart and solace in affliction; it banishes sorrow, dispels fear, nourishes our devotion and moves us to tears of repentance. What am I without it but a withered tree, a bit of dry timber to be cast into the fire? Grant, therefore, O Lord, that Your grace always go before me and be ever at my back, keeping me intent upon good works to be done, through Jesus Christ, Your Son and my Lord. Amen. (Book 3, Chapter 55)

We must consider ourselves exiles in this world.

If you wish to remain steadfast in grace and to grow in virtue, consider yourself an exile and a pilgrim in this world. You must rejoice to be considered a fool and a contemptuous person for the love of God. (Book 1, Chapter 17)

Our merit and progress in the spiritual life does not consist in the enjoyment of consolations and heavenly sweetness, but rather in bearing adversities and afflictions. (Book 2, Chapter 12)

Grace requires first submitting ourselves to God.

Those who freely give themselves to Your holy service will receive great grace. (Book 3, Chapter 10)

They who serve Me freely and willingly will receive grace for grace. (Book 3, Chapter 9)

Grace drives out envy or self-love.

If heavenly grace and true charity enter into your heart, there will be no room for envy, no narrowness of heart, nor will self-love rule you. (Book 3, Chapter 9)

God's grace is our strength and makes us rich in spirit.

How can I bear the miseries of this life without Your grace and mercy to strengthen me? Do not turn Your face from me and do not delay to visit me with Your comfort; otherwise my soul will become *like a parched land* (Ps 143:6) to You without the water of grace. (Book 3, Chapter 3)

O blessed grace, that makes the poor in spirit rich in virtue, and makes those who are endowed with worldly goods humble of heart, come and descend into my soul and fill me with Your consolation, lest my soul faint because of its own weariness and dryness! I beseech You, O Lord, that I may find favor in Your sight, for this favor of *Your grace is sufficient for me* (2 Cor 12:19), even though I lack those gifts which nature desires. I will have nothing to fear from trials and tribulations so long as Your grace is with me. It is my strength, my counsel and my help, more powerful than all my enemies, and wiser than all the worldly-wise. (Book 3, Chapter 55)

Without God's grace, we can do nothing.

From this it follows that *though I will to do good, because of my weakness I fail to accomplish it* (Rom 7:18). Thus I often make good resolutions, but because grace is lacking to me, in my weakness I often turn back and yield to the slightest resistance. (Book 3, Chapter 55)

Dear Lord, how absolutely necessary is Your grace for me, not only to begin that which is good, but to persevere with it and to accomplish it. Without You, I can do nothing, but when Your grace strengthens me, I can do all things. (Book 3, Chapter 55)

With God's grace, we can have eternal life.

Drive from our hearts, O Lord, all suspicion, perversity, anger, dissension, and whatever else may wound charity or lessen brotherly love. Be merciful, O Lord, be merciful to those who implore Your mercy; give grace to those in need;

make us all live in such a way as to be worthy to possess Your grace and life everlasting. Amen. (Book 4, Chapter 9)

Observe the contrast between nature and grace to help us understand the differences between the two and how our natural man is antithetical to God's grace.

Of the Opposition Between Nature and Grace

My child, carefully observe the actions of nature and grace, for both move in opposite directions and in such subtle ways as to be indistinguishable except by the spiritually enlightened. All human beings long after goodness and pretend there is some good in what they say or do; that is why many are deceived by an apparent goodness.

2. Nature indeed is wily and betrays many through its deceits and crafty ways, and has always self as its end. On the other hand, grace walks with simplicity, turning aside from all that appears evil. It employs no deceits, but does all unaffectedly, purely for God, in Whom it rests.

3. Nature dies hard and is not easily overcome or repressed. Never under its own accord will it be subject to obedience. But grace studies how to be mortified to both the world and the flesh, desires to be overcome and under obedience, and seeks not its own liberty, nor to dominate any creature. Grace always wants to live under God's direction,

and for His sake to place itself humbly under every human creature.

4. Nature always looks to its own advantage, considering what gain it can derive from another. But grace is not concerned with its own profit, but with what may benefit others.

5. Nature looks for honor and respect. Grace refers all honor and reverence to God.

6. Nature fears rebukes and contempt. Grace is happy to suffer them for the Name of Jesus.

7. Nature craves ease and idleness. But grace cannot be idle and gladly embraces toil.

8. Nature surrounds itself with rare and costly things and looks down upon what is coarse and cheap. Grace takes joy in humble and simple things, does not disdain hard things, nor refuses to be clad in poor clothing.

9. Nature focuses its attention on worldly matters, is elated by material gains, is downcast by losses, and is cut to the quick by a sharp word. Grace is intent upon things eternal, is not worried by the loss of things, nor grieved by the unkind word; for its treasure and joy are in heaven, where nothing is lost.

10. Nature is greedy and gladly takes rather than gives, and clings possessively to private possessions. But grace is kind and unselfish, avoids self-interest, is content with little, and rightly

judges that *it is more blessed to give than to receive* (Acts 20:35).

11. Nature is inclined to seek creatures, to the love of its own flesh, to idle pastimes and to unnecessary running about. Grace draws people toward the love of God and virtuous living, renounces all created things, flees the world, despises the lusts of the flesh, restrains all useless wanderings, and avoids as much as possible appearing in public.

12. Nature gladly receives exterior comfort to gratify the senses. Grace seeks comfort only in God, finding delight in the Sovereign Good beyond all things visible.

13. Nature does everything for personal profit, never doing any work for nothing, but always looking for repayment—at least in equal amount, if not better, or else for praise and favor—and longs to have its deeds and words highly valued. On the other hand, grace seeks no temporal reward nor any other compensation in payment, but only God Himself. Grace will have no more of the necessities of life than that which serves to obtain everlasting life.

14. Nature enjoys having a crowd of relatives and friends, prides itself on the family tree and a distinguished background. Nature flatters the rich and caters to those in power and approves those who share the same opinions as itself. But grace behaves differently, for it loves even its enemies,

JESUS GIVES US PEACE IN THE SPIRIT—"The Advocate, the Holy Spirit, Whom the Father will send in My Name, will teach you everything and remind you of all that I have said to you. Peace I leave with you, My peace I give to you" (Jn 14:26f).

TRUSTING LOVE FOR GOD—"Gaze upon the birds in the sky . . . your heavenly Father feeds them. . . . Let your main focus be on His kingdom and His righteousness, and all these things will be given to you as well" (Mt 6:26, 33).

and does not boast of having a large circle of friends. It cares not for rank or birth unless joined with greater virtue. It favors the poor rather than the rich; and has more in common with the simple and the innocent than with the influential. It rejoices with the truthful and not with liars. It encourages the good to be zealous to aim higher, and by the exercise of virtues to become more like Christ, our Lord.

15. As soon as trouble and want appear, nature is quick to complain. Grace gladly bears poverty with constancy.

16. Nature refers all things to itself and all its striving is for itself but grace refers all things back to God, Who is their Source. Grace is not presumptuous and attributes no good to self; neither does grace argue or prefer its own opinions, but submits to Eternal Wisdom.

17. Nature wants to know secrets and is avid for news, wants to appear in public and to try out new things. It likes to be noticed and to do sensational things to win approval. Grace cares nothing for the novel or curious, for it knows that all this springs from our old corruption, since there is nothing new or lasting upon earth. Grace teaches us to control our senses, to shun all vain pleasure and outward show, and humbly to hide anything that might win human admiration. In all knowledge and in all actions, grace seeks not only spiritual profit, but, above all, the praise and honor of

God, that He may be blessed in His gifts, which He freely bestows through His love.

18. This grace is a supernatural light and a special gift of God. It is the proper mark of the elect and a pledge of eternal salvation. It lifts a person above the things of earth to the love of heavenly things, making a spiritual person of a worldling. The more nature is kept down and overcome, the more grace fills a human soul, and through new daily visitations the soul is formed more and more to the image of God. (Book 3, Chapter 54)

CHAPTER 10

Gratitude

When Jesus entered a certain village, ten men who were lepers called out to Him to have mercy on them. Jesus cleansed them all. One of them came back and gave Jesus thanks. But Jesus wondered where the other nine were. (Lk 17:12-17). Gratitude is a trait that characterizes a disciple of Jesus Christ. Thomas urged his readers to remember what God has given each of them, and that, without gratitude, God's gift of grace cannot come. We must be grateful in adversity, and even when we feel the Lord is not consoling us. Ultimately, it is God who gives us everything, Thomas writes. We must be grateful to God "who deals so generously with you, mercifully visits you, fervently stirs you and powerfully raises you up, so that you do not revert back to the things of earth."

Be grateful for what God gives us because it is not our due, but His gift.

[W]hen God sends you spiritual comfort, accept it gladly and thank Him for it, but fully realize that it is God's mercy that sends it and not any deserving of yours. (Book 2, Chapter 9)

Be grateful for whatever the Lord gives us, no matter what it is.

Be grateful, therefore, for the least gift and you will be worthy to receive more. Regard the least gift as the greatest and the most contemptible as a special prize. For if you consider the dignity of the Giver, no favor will seem small or valueless. Nothing is small that comes from the Most High God. Indeed, even if He sends punishment and affliction, we should accept it with gratitude; for whatever He permits to happen to us is always with our salvation in view. (Book 2, Chapter 10)

Lord, I willingly bear for You whatever You are pleased to give me. With indifference I will take from Your hand good and bad, bitter and sweet, joy and sorrow; and for all these things that may happen to me, I thank You with all my heart. (Book 3, Chapter 17)

When we are not grateful, we cannot receive God's gifts.

God does well in sending the grace of comfort, but human beings do ill in not returning all to God with thanks. Therefore, these gifts of grace cannot flow in us because of our ingratitude to the

Giver in not returning all to Him, the Source. Grace is always given to the person who is grateful, and God readily gives to the humble what is taken from the proud. (Book 2, Chapter 10)

My child, when you feel the desire for eternal happiness given to you from above, so that you wish to abandon this mortal body in order to behold clearly and without any shadow the brightness of My glory, open wide your heart, and with all the desire of your soul receive this holy inspiration. Give greatest thanks to the good God, Who deals so generously with you, mercifully visits you, fervently stirs you and powerfully raises you up, so that you do not revert back to the things of earth. (Book 3, Chapter 49)

They who love Jesus purely for Himself and not for their own sake bless Him in all trouble and anguish as well as in time of consolation. Even if He never sent them consolation, they would still praise Him and give thanks. (Book 2, Chapter 11)

I thank You, O heavenly Father, that You have not spared my sins, that Your rod of correction has taught me by inflicting pains and by sending afflictions both within and without. You are the heavenly Physician, Who alone can comfort me, Who—in the midst of wounds—heals, *Who casts down to the depths of the netherworld and brings up from the great abyss* (Tob 13:2). Your tender care is upon me, and your very rod shall instruct me. (Book 3, Chapter 50)

CHAPTER 11

Humility

One of the most prominent themes in *The Imitation of Christ* is the need to be humble. Humility is the mark of a disciple of Christ. But Thomas offered specific guidance on the benefits of humility, particularly as a tool for bringing us closer to God. He also explained how frailty and weakness are good for the soul because they remind us to be humble. Ultimately, it is our humility that will bring us salvation and return us to God.

Too often, we are inclined not to be humble.

We cannot count on ourselves much, for often through lack of grace and understanding our judgment is a limited one and we soon lose what we have through our own neglect. Often we are unaware of our own interior blindness. Many times we do evil and, what is far worse, we justify it. Sometimes our passions rule us and we mistake it for zeal. We are critical of the small defects in our neighbors, but overlook the serious faults in ourselves. We are quick to complain of what we put up with from others, with never a thought of what others suffer from us. If we would see ourselves as we really are, we would not find cause to judge others severely. Those who are turned to God consider the care of themselves before all other cares; and looking seriously to themselves, they find it easy to be silent about the deeds of others. (Book 2, Chapter 5)

Don't be boastful or vain or God will be displeased.

Do not boast of riches if you have them, or of your important friends; but glory in God only, from Whom all good things come and Who, being the highest good, desires to give us Himself. Do not boast of beauty of body, which is soon disfigured by illness or age. Do not be proud of any talents or skills you possess, for in this way you displease God from Whom you have received them. Do not consider yourself better than others, for you may be worse in God's sight. Do not be proud of your good works, for often what pleases us displeases God, Whose judgments differ from the judgment of humans. Whatever goodness or virtue is in you, believe that your neighbor has better qualities; in this way you will preserve humility. (Book 1, Chapter 7)

Don't be proud.

Do not be proud of your good works, for often what pleases us displeases God, Whose judgments differ from the judgment of humans. Whatever goodness or virtue is in you, believe that your neighbor has better qualities; in this way you will preserve humility. It will not hurt you to consider yourself worse than others, even if this is not really so; but it will hurt greatly if you prefer yourself above another, although that person might be a great sinner. A humble person is a peaceful person; but the hearts of the proud are full of envy and resentment. (Book 1, Chapter 7)

Always to do the best you can and to make little of yourself is the mark of a humble soul. (Book 2, Chapter 6)

From now on, therefore, I will make myself completely insignificant and more earnestly seek You; for You, Lord Jesus, deal with me far above what I deserve—indeed far above all that I dare to ask or hope for. (Book 3, Chapter 8)

Associate with the humble and simple.

[D]o not flatter the rich, or seek to be in the presence of the great without good reason. Rather associate yourself with those who are humble and have simplicity, who are devout and self-disciplined, talking with them about those things that will edify and strengthen the soul. (Book 1, Chapter 8)

Temptations can make us humble.

No one in this world is so perfect or holy as not to have temptations sometimes. We can never be entirely free of them. Sometimes these temptations can be very severe and troublesome, but if we resist them, they will be very useful to us; for by experiencing them we are humbled, cleansed and instructed. (Book 1, Chapter 13)

As frail people, we have good reason to be humble.

How frail is human nature that we are always inclined to evil! Today you confess your sins and tomorrow you commit the same ones again. Now you resolve to be vigilant, with all good intention to persevere, and shortly after you act as if you never had a good intention. We have good reason to humble ourselves and never to have a good opinion of ourselves, since we are so weak and unstable. The virtue we strove by grace to gain may soon be lost through carelessness. (Book 1, Chapter 22)

Don't become boastful or overconfident when blessed, but remain humble.

However, when God sends you spiritual comfort, accept it gladly and thank Him for it, but fully realize that it is God's mercy that sends it and not any deserving of yours. Do not be proud, presumptuous or overjoyed; rather let this gift humble you and be wary and fearful in all you do; for surely that time will pass away and be followed by temptation. (Book 2, Chapter 9)

Persons who have received more cannot boast as though they had gained it by their own merit, nor consider themselves above others, nor look down on those who have received less; for those are greater and more acceptable to You who attribute less to themselves, returning humble and devout thanks to You. Those who, through humility, consider themselves the least and most unworthy of all are fit to receive still greater blessings. (Book 3, Chapter 22)

Trials bring humility.

God wants you to learn to suffer tribulation without comfort and, submitting yourself entirely to Him, to grow in humility through tribulation. (Book 2, Chapter 12)

I am more pleased, My child, when you are patient and humble under adversity than when you feel devout and consoled in prosperity. Why are you so upset when someone says an unkind word about you? It could have been worse, but even so, you should not let it disturb you. Forget about it; it is not the first, or anything new; and it will not be the last, if you live long enough. You are so courageous as long as no opposition comes your way. You also can give good advice and can encourage others with your words; but when some unexpected trouble turns up on your own doorstep, your good advice and moral support fail you. Think over your great frailty which you often experience in such trifling difficulties. Yet it is for your spiritual help that these and similar things are permitted to happen to you. (Book 3, Chapter 57)

Take the humblest place and avoid vainglory.

Always set yourself in the lowest place (Lk 14:10), and you will be given the highest; for the highest cannot exist without the lowest. The Saints who are highest in God's sight are the least in their own; and the more glorious they are, the more humble they are in heart, full of truth and heavenly joy and not desirous of vainglory. Being grounded and confirmed in God, they can in no way be proud. They who ascribe to God whatever good they have received do not seek glory from one another, but only that glory which is from God; and the desire of their hearts is that God be praised in Himself and in all His Saints, and to this end they always tend. (Book 2, Chapter 10)

The humble are the friends and acquaintances of the Lord.

Lord, I count it as a benefit not to have those gifts which others can see and for which I might be complimented and praised. Furthermore, although persons should consider their own poverty and worthlessness, they should not be grieved or depressed, but rather they should feel happy and consoled; for You daily choose the humble and those who are despised by the world to be Your special friends and servants. (Book 3, Chapter 22)

Don't be envious of others, but remember humility.

My child, do not take it to heart if you see others honored and promoted, and yourself despised and looked down upon. Raise up your heart to Me in heaven, and the contempt of people on earth will not sadden you. (Book 3, Chapter 41)

God is with the humble and blesses them.

Be humble and peaceful and Jesus will be with you. (Book 2, Chapter 8)

My child, *walk before Me in truth* (1 Ki 2:4) and simplicity of heart—without pretense. Those who so walk will be shielded from the attacks of the evil one; and Truth shall free them from deceivers and the detractions of evil people. (Book 3, Chapter 4)

When you admit your faults, you easily pacify others and reconcile yourself with those you have offended. God never refuses the humble; rather He delivers and comforts them and fills them with His grace. He also opens to them the secrets of His Heart and draws them to Himself, raising them to the heights of glory because of their humility. (Book 2, Chapter 2)

Submit yourself humbly to God, and submit your senses to faith, and the light of knowledge will be given to you for your spiritual well-being, according to the measure of God. (Book 4, Chapter 18)

God walks with the simple, makes Himself known to the humble, and gives understanding to the poor in spirit. He reveals His meaning to the clean of heart, but He hides His grace from the proud and curious. (Book 4, Chapter 18)

The humble are at peace because they trust God.

Humble people are always at peace, even when they are put to shame, because they trust in God and not in the world. (Book 2, Chapter 2)

Humility brings obedience, wisdom, and peace.

If you are humble and submissive to God's will, you will have peace in all you do. (Book 1, Chapter 4)

Salvation and exaltation come to the humble in spirit.

Let us humbly submit ourselves to God in all trials and temptations; for *it is the humble and submissive that He will save and exalt* (Ps 34:19). (Book 1, Chapter 13)

If you want to be exalted in heaven, humble yourself on earth. (Book 3, Chapter 56)

The humble will receive the kingdom of God.

Woe to them who disdain to humble themselves willingly as little children; for the gate of the heavenly kingdom is low, and will not permit them to enter. Woe also to the rich who have their comforts in this world. The poor will enter into the kingdom of God, while the rich stand lamenting outside. So rejoice, you who are humble and poor in spirit. It is to you that the kingdom of God belongs—provided you walk steadfastly in the way of truth. (Book 3, Chapter 58)

CHRIST'S COMING IN GLORY—"Then the sign of the Son of Man will appear in heaven, and all the peoples of earth will mourn, and they will see the Son of Man coming on the clouds of heaven with power and great glory" (Mt 24:30).

JESUS INVITES US TO DIALOGUE WITH HIM—"I have called you friends, because I have revealed to you everything that I have heard from My Father. You did not choose Me. Rather, I chose you" (Jn 15:15f).

CHAPTER 12

Judgment

The Savior admonished the disciples to "judge not" (Mt 7:1). Judging is God's task and not ours. Yet, we are inclined to question God's judgment and substitute it for our own. Thomas addressed our human tendency of judging others and also questioning God's judgment.

We do not understand God's judgment so we must leave matters of judgment in His hands.

My child, you must beware of disputing about matters above your understanding, or about the hidden judgments of God. Do not wonder why one man is forsaken by God, while another receives an abundance of His grace; why this person has so much trouble and the other is so greatly advanced. These things surpass our comprehension and no mere human discourse can explain the divine judgments. Therefore, when the devil suggests questions to you, or curious people inquire about them, simply reply in the words of the Prophet: *You are righteous, O Lord, and Your judgments are right* (Ps 119:137). Or you can say: *The ordinances of the Lord are true, and all of them are just* (Ps 19:10). My judgments are to be feared, for they are beyond the scope of human reason. (Book 3, Chapter 58)

Righteous persons are never dismayed by anything I permit to happen to them. Although they be wrongly accused, it will not worry them much; neither will they be overjoyed if they be reasonably acquitted. They know that *I am the searcher of all hearts* (Rev 2:23), Who judge not according to outward appearances or by the way things look to humans, but by what I esteem praiseworthy. (Book 3, Chapter 46)

Be careful about trusting in the judgment of others; be patient with unjust judgments by others.

My child, firmly cling to the Lord and do not fear the judgments of humans, when your conscience assures you that you seek to be devout and innocent. Consider it a good thing and rejoice when you suffer that way. It will not be burdensome to you if you are humble of heart, nor if you trust more in God than in yourself. A lot of people utter many things; therefore attach little importance to what they say. Neither is it possible to satisfy everybody. St. Paul tried to please everyone in the Lord and became all things to all. Nevertheless, he paid little attention to being judged by humans.

He worked for the formation and salvation of others, as much as he could and found possible. In spite of all that, he was unable to prevent others from sometimes judging or despising him.

Therefore he committed everything to God, Who is all-knowing, and put on the armor of patience and humility against the onslaughts of evil tongues, or against those who thought or expressed vain or bad things about him. Sometimes, however, he answered his accusers, when his silence might scandalize the weak.

Why be afraid of mortals? A human being is here today and gone tomorrow. Keep up a wholesome fear of God and you will not find it necessary to be afraid of humans. What can others really do against you by words and insults? Those who thus attack you hurt themselves more than you, and wherever they may be, they will not escape God's judgment. (Book 3, Chapter 36)

God's judgment is true and correct, despite what men say.

Human judgment is often erroneous. My judgment is true; it shall stand and can never be overthrown. To many it remains hidden, and only to a few is it made manifest; yet it never errs, nor can it err, though to the unwise it may appear wrong. (Book 3, Chapter 46)

Trust in God rather than our own judgment.

But if you do not keep your eyes fixed on God, nor keep Him in your heart, then you will be easily upset by the slightest rebuke. Those who trust in Me and rely not on their own judgment will fear no human. For I am the Judge and the Discerner of all secrets. (Book 3, Chapter 46)

We must be careful in judging since we often are unable to do so wisely.

Our own opinions and lack of knowledge often lead us astray, because we do not know the truth as it is. (Book 1, Chapter 3)

We should avoid judging others and thinking ourselves better.

Watch over yourself and take care not to judge the actions of other people. We gain nothing by criticizing others, but often are mistaken and thereby offend God. But to judge yourself and your own actions is always profitable. We often judge a thing according to our preference and therefore our judgment is emotional rather than objective. This stubbornness in our own opinions would not dominate our judgments if our hearts were set on God. (Book 1, Chapter 14)

Nothing is so beneficial as a true knowledge of ourselves, which produces a wholesome self-contempt. Always think kindly of others, while holding yourself as nothing; this is true wisdom and leads to perfection. If you see another commit a grievous sin, or whose faults are flagrant, do not regard yourself as better, for you do not know what you would do if similarly tempted. You are in good disposition now, but you do not know how long you will persevere in it. Always keep in mind that all are frail, but none so frail as yourself. (Book 1, Chapter 2)

We should not hold others to a higher standard than ourselves. If we look at our own faults, we will not severely judge others.

Often we are unaware of our own interior blindness. Many times we do evil and, what is far worse, we justify it. Sometimes our passions rule us and we mistake it for zeal. We are critical of the small defects in our neighbors, but overlook the serious faults in ourselves. We are quick to complain of what we put up with from others, with never a thought of what others suffer from us. If we would see ourselves as we really are, we would not find cause to judge others severely. (Book 2, Chapter 5)

At Judgment Day, we will be judged on how we have lived.

On the day of judgment we will not be asked what we have read, but what we have done; neither will we be asked how well we have spoken, but how devoutly we have lived. (Book 1, Chapter 3)

In all things look to the end and how you will appear before the strict Judge. Nothing is hidden from Him; neither will He accept bribes, nor receive excuses. He will judge all things rightly and truly. Wretched sinner that you are, what answer will you then give your God, Who knows all your evil deeds, when here you are afraid to face an angry human being? Why do you not provide for that day of judgment now, since there will be no one to defend or make excuses for you, for everyone will have enough to do to answer for oneself?

Now you can gain merit; your tears and sighs are heard and your sorrow and repentance acceptable. (Book 1, Chapter 24)

CHAPTER 13

Knowledge

Many are proud of the university degrees they hold and the knowledge those degrees suggest. Thomas reminded us that such knowledge is less important than knowledge of God. We must be careful not to think too much of our own knowledge and assume we know so very much. We also should be careful what divine knowledge we seek to attain; knowledge brings with it responsibility and a need to act rather than just to know. Importantly, when we search for divine knowledge, it must not be to appear learned and gratify our pride but to remind us of our sins and draw us closer to God.

Divine knowledge and grace are more important than scholarly knowledge.

There is a vast difference between the wisdom of an enlightened and devout soul and the knowledge of a learned and studious scholar. The knowledge which is poured into the soul by the influence of God's grace is far nobler than that which is acquired by human labor and study. (Book 3, Chapter 31)

Knowledge is a natural desire in all people. But knowledge for its own sake is useless unless you fear God. An unlearned peasant, whose contentment is the service of God, is far better than the learned and the clever, whose pride in their knowledge leads them to neglect their souls while fixing their attention on the stars. (Book 1, Chapter 2)

An overweening desire for knowledge brings many distractions and much delusion. Many like to be considered learned and to be praised for their wisdom; how much knowledge there is which adds nothing to the good of the soul! To spend yourself on worldly pursuits which do nothing to further your eternal salvation is unwise. It is useless to spend much time in talking; only a holy life and a good conscience will ease your mind and satisfy your soul, enabling you to face God with confidence. (Book 1, Chapter 2)

Lofty words neither save you nor make you a Saint; only a virtuous life makes you dear to God. It is better to experience contrition than to be able to define it. To be well versed in Scripture and all the sayings of philosophers will not profit you if you are without God's love and His grace. (Book 1, Chapter 1)

We will be judged according to the knowledge we have.

Remember, the more you know, the more severely you will be judged. So do not be proud of any skill or knowledge you may have, for such is an awesome responsibility. (Book 1, Chapter 2)

Our knowledge on this earth is limited. We don't know what may happen in the future.

The hour of death will soon come for you. See to it that you spend your time here well. There is a common saying that human beings are here today and gone tomorrow. And once they are out of sight, they are soon forgotten. How dull we are and hard of heart, for we think only of the present and make little provision for the life hereafter! If you were wise, you would so order your life as though you were to die before the day is over. If your conscience were clear, you would not be afraid of death. Better to give up sin than to fear death. If you are unprepared to face death today, how will you be tomorrow? Tomorrow is uncertain and you may not be here to see it. (Book 1, Chapter 23)

We must not think what we see here or what is valued here is all there is.

They are wise who observe things as they are and not by what is said about them, or by the value put on them; for they are taught by God and not by humans. (Book 2, Chapter 1)

It is important to know the difference between visible and spiritual knowledge.

Grant me, O Lord, to know what I ought to know, to love what I ought to love, to esteem what is valuable to You, and to loathe what is vile in Your eyes. Let me never judge according to outward appearances, nor pass judgment on the hearsay of the unwise. Matters both visible and spiritual are to be determined with right judgment; and above all let me ever seek Your goodwill and pleasure. (Book 3, Chapter 50)

Look for truth, regardless of the learning of the source.

Be concerned only with the pure truth in what you read and not with the greatness or lack of learning of the author. Think more of what is said than of the one who said it. (Book 1, Chapter 5)

A knowledge of self is the way to God.

[A] humble self-knowledge is a surer way to God than a search after deep learning. It is not wrong to pursue learning, for since it comes from God it is good as far as it goes; but it is far better to have a clean conscience and lead a virtuous life. Because some prefer to be learned than to be virtuous, they make many mistakes and produce little or no fruit. (Book 1, Chapter 3)

Trust not your own cleverness nor your own point of view.

Do not trust your own cleverness nor that of any person; rather, put your trust in the grace of God, Who gives aid to the humble but humiliates the presumptuous. (Book 1, Chapter 7)

In reality, all of us are inclined to do our own will and agree more readily with those who hold with our views. But if we want to have the presence of God among us, then we must be willing to give up our own way in order to live in love and harmony with others. Surely there are no persons so wise that they know everything. Therefore, listen to the opinions of others and do not trust too much in your own point of view. Perhaps you are right, but by setting aside your own will and following another out of love for God, you will profit by it. (Book 1, Chapter 9)

Be humble about your knowledge.

No matter how much you know, realize how much there is that you do not know. Do not be afraid to acknowledge your own ignorance. Why have an exalted opinion of yourself when you know there are many, even in your own field, whose knowledge surpasses yours? If you want to learn anything worthwhile, seek rather to be unknown and to be thought of as nothing. (Book 1, Chapter 2)

Don't favor a search for mysteries over salvation.

There are some who are not sincere in their conduct with Me, but, led by curiosity and pride to search the mysteries of God, neglect themselves and their spiritual welfare. Such people often fall into grave temptations and sins because of their pride and curiosity. (Book 3, Chapter 4)

Do not read scriptures to surpass others in knowledge, but to find what will change you inwardly.

Reading the Scriptures to appear more learned will not benefit you; but rather study how to overcome your worst faults. This will profit you more than having the answers to difficult questions at your fingertips. (Book 3, Chapter 43)

Knowledge without the love of God will not do us much good.

If your knowledge encompasses the universe and the love of God is not in you, what good will it do you in God's sight? (Book 1, Chapter 2)

Knowledge must be accompanied by action.

My child, since you know these things and have read about them, you will be blessed if you put them into practice. *Anyone who has received My commandments and observes them is the one who loves Me. . . . I will love and reveal Myself to such a one* (Jn 14:21); and I will make that person sit down with Me in the kingdom of My Father. (Book 3, Chapter 56)

CHAPTER 14

Liberty

Jesus promised the disciples that "you shall know the truth, and the truth shall make you free" (Jn 8:32). Freedom or liberty is a highly-coveted state for human beings. We wish to do what we want and be unencumbered. Yet, it is our submissiveness to God rather than the absence of rules or regulations or commitments that makes us free. Thomas à Kempis explained that it is our covenant to surrender our will and to serve God and others that offers true liberty. He enumerated what we must do to be free: eschew worldly things, cast off vanity, and be willing to sacrifice our own will in order to follow God.

Our own liberty comes from loving and serving God and others.

If your main object is the will of God and the good of your neighbor, you will have great interior freedom. (Book 2, Chapter 4)

Those who love Jesus and the truth, who lead an interior life free from unruly affections, can turn to God at will, lift themselves up in spirit and repose in Christ with joy. (Book 2, Chapter 1)

Liberty comes from following the straight and narrow way and not from worldly things.

It is a great honor to serve You, and to despise all things for love of You. Those who freely give themselves to Your holy service will receive great grace. (Book 3, Chapter 10)

If we wish true liberty, we must give up our will and be humble.

My child, now I shall teach you the way of true peace and perfect liberty.

Dear Lord, do as You say, for it will be a joy for me to hear this.

Try, my child, to do the will of another rather than your own. Always choose to have fewer riches rather than more. Always seek the lowest place and desire to be subject to all. Always wish for and pray that the will of God be accomplished in you. Such a person enters into the abode of true peace and inward rest. (Book 3, Chapter 23)

Perfect liberty comes with our willingness to sacrifice to obtain the things of Jesus Christ.

My child, you cannot have perfect freedom unless you wholly renounce yourself. Those who think only of themselves and are lovers of themselves; the covetous, the curious, the pretentious, the pleasure-seekers—concerned with their own comforts and not the interests of Jesus Christ; those who plan and pursue the things which cannot last—are bound with chains of their own making. Whatever does not come from God will perish entirely. (Book 3, Chapter 32)

There are some who commit themselves, but with some restrictions; for they do not trust God fully and so they are busy providing for themselves. Some at first give up everything; but afterward, under the pressure of temptation, they return to what they had forsaken; and so they do not advance in virtue. Such persons will not acquire the true liberty of one who is clean of heart, nor will they obtain the grace of a most joyful familiarity with Me. To attain this, they must first wholly renounce themselves and daily offer themselves as victims of sacrifice to Me; for without this there cannot exist any lasting divine union. (Book 3, Chapter 37)

To be free, we must make God the center of our lives.

Iron cast into the fire loses its rust and becomes clean and bright; and those who make God the center of their lives are cleansed of slothfulness and are changed into new persons. The moment you begin to grow lukewarm, everything is a big effort and you willingly receive distractions from without. But as soon as you begin to conquer yourself and walk uprightly in the way of God, then the effort expended seems little which before you thought was insurmountable. (Book 2, Chapter 4)

Liberty does not come from pursuit of earthly things.

Live on earth as a pilgrim and a stranger, unconcerned with the world's business. Let your heart remain free and lifted up to God, for you have not here a lasting city. (Book 1, Chapter 23)

PROOF OF TRUE LOVE—"A woman in the crowd called out to Him and said, 'Blessed is the womb that bore You. . . .' Jesus replied, 'Blessed, rather, are those who hear the word of God and obey it' " (Lk 11:27f).

JESUS TELLS US TO SERVE GOD AND SPURN SATAN—"Depart from My sight, Satan! . . . 'You shall worship the Lord your God; and Him alone shall you serve' " (Mt 4:10f).

Nor does liberty come from heeding the vanity of others.

If Truth makes you free, you will be free indeed and the vain words of human beings will not bother you. (Book 3, Chapter 4)

Freedom is not the result of worldly cares or seeking our own pleasure.

Why do you languish in useless grief, or why are you so worn with needless cares? Resign yourself to My will and you will suffer no loss. If you look for this thing or that, or wish to be in this place or that, simply for your own advantage or pleasure, you will never be at rest, nor free from anxiety. You will find something to dislike in everything, and there will be someone who will cross you no matter where you are. (Book 3, Chapter 27)

CHAPTER 15

Love of God

Jesus said that loving God is the first and greatest commandment (Mt 22:37). But how does one love God? What happens when we love God? In his first epistle in the New Testament, John explained that God loved us first (1 Jn 4:19). What is that love that God has for us? What does it mean for our lives? Is it temporary or lasting?

These are questions Thomas à Kempis pondered and sought to answer. The passages below from *The Imitation of Christ* are his answers to those questions and others related to what God's love is and how and why we should love God in return.

We find ourselves by loving God.

Lord, Your love is the cause of this, which goes before me and helps me in all my necessities; it protects me from those grave dangers to which I am most prone to succumb. I have lost You and myself, too, by my disordered self-love; by seeking You again, I found both You and myself. (Book 3, Chapter 8)

God's love is lasting and He will not forsake us.

[T]hose who always cling to Jesus will stand firm forever. Love Him and keep Him for your friend; for when all others forsake you, He will not leave you nor let you perish in the end. (Book 2, Chapter 7)

God's love will comfort and refresh us.

Whatever I can desire or imagine for my comfort, I do not expect here but hereafter. If I alone should have all the comforts of this world and could enjoy all its pleasures according to my own desire and without sin, it is certain that they could not last long. Therefore my soul can never be fully comforted, nor be perfectly refreshed except in God, the comforter of the poor in spirit and the refuge of the humble. (Book 3, Chapter 16)

Whatever we love, that is what we think about and talk about and carry home with us.

But You, O Eternal Truth, have plainly told us: *"Where your treasure is, there will your heart also be"* (Mt 6:21). So, if I love heaven, I love to think of heavenly things; but if I love the world, I rejoice at its prosperity and grieve over its adversity. If I love the spirit, I delight to think of spiritual things; but if I love the flesh my imagination is occupied with the delights of the flesh. So whatever is uppermost in my affections, these I willingly listen to and speak of, and carry the thoughts of them often in my mind. Blessed are those who abandon all things. (Book 3, Chapter 48)

To love God, we must be willing to endure.

You must be willing to suffer all things gladly for the love of God: labors, sorrows, temptations, afflictions; all anxieties, needs, infirmities, injuries, detraction, rebukes; all humiliations, confusions, corrections, and contempt. Such things are aids to virtue and test those who are in the service of Christ, preparing them for a heavenly crown. For this short labor I will give an eternal reward, and for passing confusion, infinite glory. (Book 3, Chapter 35)

Steel yourself, as a faithful servant of Christ, bravely to bear the cross of your Lord, Who out of love for you was nailed to the cross. Prepare yourself, then, to suffer all kinds of adversities and inconveniences in this wretched life; for you cannot avoid them no matter where you go, and they will find you no matter where you hide. So it is in life, and there is no avenue of escape but to keep yourself in patience. If you desire to be our Lord's dear friend and to share what is His, then you must drink heartily of His chalice. As for consolations, leave those to His will and He will arrange them as He sees best for you. (Book 2, Chapter 12)

Christ's love for us never diminishes and His atonement on our behalf is never ended.

Christ's love for us never diminishes, nor is the greatness of His atonement ever consumed. (Book 4, Chapter 2)

The traits of a love of God.

Love is swift, sincere, pious, joyful and glad; it is strong, patient, faithful, wise, forbearing, courageous, and is never self-seeking; for when people seek themselves, they cease to love. Love is cautious, humble and upright; not weak, not flighty, nor concerned with trifles. It is sober, chaste, firm, quiet, and keeps guard over the senses. Love is submissive and obedient to authority, mean and despicable in its own sight, devout and thankful to God. Love always trusts and hopes in God, even when it lacks fervor; for there is no living in love without some sorrow or pain. (Book 3, Chapter 5)

Nothing is sweeter than love, nothing higher, nothing stronger, nothing larger, nothing more joyful, nothing fuller, nothing better in heaven or on earth; for love is born of God and can find its rest only in God above all He has created. Such lovers fly high, run swiftly and rejoice. Their souls are free; they give all for all and have all in all. For they rest in One Supreme Goodness above all things, from Whom all other good flows and proceeds. They look not only at the gifts, but at the Giver, Who is above all gifts.

Love knows no limits, but is fervent above all measure. It feels no burden, makes light of labor, desiring to do more than it is able. Nothing is impossible to love, for it thinks that it can and may do all things for the Beloved. Therefore it does and effects many things, while those who do not love falter and fail.

Love is ever watchful; it rests, but does not sleep; though weary, it is not tired; restricted, yet not hindered. Although it sees reason to fear, it is not dismayed; but like a spark of fire or a burning flame, it blazes upward to God by the fervor of its love, and through the help of His grace is delivered from all dangers. Those who love thus know well what their voices mean when they cry out to God with all the ardor of their soul: You, Lord God, are my whole love and all my desire. You are all mine and I am all Yours. (Book 3, Chapter 5)

He who loves Jesus will enjoy fruitful peace.

Our Lord will visit the devout with His consolations, if they will make room for Him in the depths of their hearts. This is where He desires to be, and He will bring them many graces and much peace, and the sublime intimacy of His presence. (Book 2, Chapter 1)

If we love Jesus, we will have the love of the Father.

Lose no time, then, faithful soul, in preparing your heart to meet Christ, the Beloved, so that He may come and live in you. Does He not say: *"Whoever loves Me will keep My word, . . . We will come to him and make Our abode with him"* (Jn 14:23)? (Book 2, Chapter 1)

To love God, we must reject a love of created things.

No confidence is to be placed in mortal human beings, no matter how helpful they may be or how dear to us, for we are all frail. Neither should you be downcast if one day they are on your side and the next day they are against you; for humans are changeable like the wind. Therefore, put your complete trust in God and let Him be the center of your love and fear. He will answer for you and will do what He sees best for you. (Book 2, Chapter 1)

If you were well purified from worldly attachments, whatever happened would turn to your spiritual profit and to an increase of grace and virtue in your soul. But because of your excess love of earthly things, many things displease and annoy you. Nothing so defiles and ensnares a person's heart as the undisciplined love of created things. If you will refuse outward consolations, then you will think of heavenly things and continually give praise to Him with a joyful heart. (Book 2, Chapter 1)

The joy of the righteous comes from a love of God.

Those who love God will glory in tribulation, for their only joy is to glory in the cross of Jesus Christ, our Lord. The glory given and received by humans lasts but a little while and usually it is followed by sadness. The glory of good persons is in their own consciences, not in the praise of others. The happiness of the good is in God and of God and their joy is in the truth. Those who long for true everlasting happiness do not care for that which is temporal. Those who seek temporal glory and do not treat it with contempt have little love for the joy of heaven. Those who are indifferent to praise or blame have great tranquility of heart. (Book 2, Chapter 6)

To love Jesus, we must follow Him regardless of the cost of discipleship.

Jesus has many lovers of His heavenly kingdom, but few cross-bearers. Many desire His consolation, but few His tribulation. Many will sit down with Him at table, but few will share His fast. All desire to rejoice with Him, but few will suffer for Him. Many will follow Him to the breaking of the bread, but few will drink the bitter cup of His Passion. Many revere His miracles, but few follow the shame of His cross. Many love Jesus when all goes well with them, and praise Him when He does them a favor; but if Jesus conceals Himself and leaves them for a little while, they fall to complaining or become depressed. They who love Jesus purely for Himself and not for their own sake bless Him in all trouble and anguish as well as in time of consolation.

Even if He never sent them consolation, they would still praise Him and give thanks. Oh how powerful is the pure love of Jesus, when not mixed with self-interest or self-love! (Book 2, Chapter 11)

We should pray to relish and love God above all things.

Give me Your heavenly wisdom, O Lord, that I may learn that the most important thing is to seek You and to find You and, above all things else, to love You. Help me to understand all other things as they truly are, according to Your wisdom. (Book 3, Chapter 27)

God loves us despite our unworthiness and weakness in loving Him.

May You be blessed, O Heavenly Father, Father of my Lord, Jesus Christ, because You have consented to be mindful of me, poor sinner that I am. O Father of mercies and God of all comfort, I thank You that sometimes You are pleased to console me with Your gracious presence, though I am unworthy of such consolation. I bless You and glorify You always, together with Your Son and the Holy Spirit, the Comforter, forever and ever. O my Lord, God, most faithful Lover, when You come into my heart, my whole being is filled with joy. You are my glory and the joy of my heart; *my hope and refuge in the time of tribulation* (Ps 59:17).

You know how weak in love and imperfect in virtue I am and how much I stand in need of Your strength and comfort. Please, Lord, visit me often and instruct me in Your holy teachings. Deliver me from evil passions and heal my heart from all disorderly affections, so that being healed inwardly and well purified, I may become ready to love You, strong to suffer for You, and firm to persevere. (Book 3, Chapter 5)

The love of Jesus moves us to do great works and desire greater perfection.

Love is a strong force—a great good in every way; it alone can make our burdens light, and alone it bears in equal balance what is pleasing and displeasing. It carries a burden and does not feel it; it makes all that is bitter taste sweet. The noble love of Jesus urges us to do great things and spurs us on to desire perfection. Love tends upward to God and is not occupied with the things of earth. Love also will be free from all worldly affections, so that its inner vision does not become dimmed, nor does it let itself be trapped by any temporal interest or downcast by misfortune. Nothing is sweeter than love, nothing higher, nothing stronger, nothing larger, nothing more joyful, nothing fuller, nothing better in heaven or on earth; for love is born of God and can find its rest only in God above all He has created. (Book 3, Chapter 5)

CHAPTER 16

Love of Others

The second great commandment is to love our neighbors as ourselves (Mt 22:39). When the lawyer asked Jesus who was his neighbor, Jesus answered with a parable that taught him (and us) that the command to "love our neighbor" is not limited to those who are geographically proximate to us. It is for universal application.

But how do we do that? Thomas placed the command to love others in practical terms. To him, it was not just an abstract concept as it was to the lawyer who approached Jesus. Rather, he sought to apply it to real-life situations. These included dealing with others who may be difficult, avoiding arguments, removing from ourselves a spirit of anger or contention towards others, and being willing to accept others.

We cannot hate others and love them at the same time.

Drive from our hearts, O Lord, all suspicion, perversity, anger, dissension, and whatever else may wound charity or lessen brotherly love. (Book 4, Chapter 9)

We should not only love our brothers and sisters, but also not consider ourselves better than them. Instead, we should show compassion and acceptance to others.

We want to have others strictly reprimanded for their offenses, but we will not be reprimanded ourselves. We are inclined to think the other person has too much liberty, but we ourselves will not put up with any restraint. There must be rules for everyone else, but we must be given free rein. It is seldom that we consider our neighbor equally with ourselves. If everyone was perfect, what would we have to endure for the love of God?

God wills us to learn to bear one another's burdens. No one is without faults, no one without a cross, no one self-sufficient and no one wise enough all alone. Therefore, we must support, comfort and assist one another, instructing and admonishing one another in all charity. (Book 1, Chapter 16)

Avoid arguing with others, even if by doing so it appears they have conquered.

It is also more profitable for you to look the other way from such things as displease you, leaving to everyone to hold the opinion that seems best, rather than to enter into heated disputes. If you are concerned only with God's view in the matter and are pleasing in His sight, you will consider it a small thing to be worsted in an argument. (Book 3, Chapter 44)

Recognize the value of others' opinions and be willing to accept others' views.

Therefore, listen to the opinions of others and do not trust too much in your own point of view. Perhaps you are right, but by setting aside your own will and following another out of love for God, you will profit by it. (Book 1, Chapter 9)

Loving others includes living with and accepting those who seem unlovable.

Look at yourself and see how far you are from real charity and humility, which cannot be resentful against anyone but oneself. It is no test of virtue to be on good terms with easy-going people, for they are always well liked. And, of course, all of us want to live in peace and prefer those who agree with us.

But the real test of virtue and deserving of praise is to live at peace with the perverse, or the aggressive and those who contradict us, for this needs a great grace. There are some contented people who can live peaceably with others; and some there are who can neither have peace themselves nor leave others in peace. They are a cross to others, but a heavier cross to themselves. There are also some who can remain at peace themselves and seek to establish peace among others. However, in this mortal life, our peace consists in the humble bearing of suffering and contradictions, not in being free of them, for we cannot live in this world without adversity. Those who can best suffer will enjoy the most peace, for

COMPLETE TRUST IN JESUS—"The centurion replied [to Jesus], 'Lord, I am not worthy to have You come under my roof. But simply say the word and my servant will be healed. . . .' Jesus said to the centurion, 'Return home. Your petition has been granted because of your faith' " (Mt 8:8, 13).

JESUS CONFORMS TO GOD'S WILL—"When the days for their purification were completed according to the law of Moses, they brought [Jesus] up to Jerusalem to present Him to the Lord" (Lk 2:22).

such persons are masters of themselves, lords of the world, with Christ for their friend, and heaven as their reward. (Book 2, Chapter 3)

Love of others includes patience with others' faults.

Learn how to be patient in enduring the faults of others, remembering that you yourself have many which others have to put up with. If you cannot make yourself be what you would like, how can you expect another to be as you would like? We wish to see perfection in others, but do not correct our own faults. We want to have others strictly reprimanded for their offenses, but we will not be reprimanded ourselves. We are inclined to think the other person has too much liberty, but we ourselves will not put up with any restraint. There must be rules for everyone else, but we must be given free rein. It is seldom that we consider our neighbor equally with ourselves. If everyone was perfect, what would we have to endure for the love of God?

God wills us to learn to bear one another's burdens. No one is without faults, no one without a cross, no one self-sufficient and no one wise enough all alone. Therefore, we must support, comfort and assist one another, instructing and admonishing one another in all charity. (Book 1, Chapter 16)

We should focus on love and not material things.

Wise lovers do not consider the gift of the Lover as much as they do the love of the Giver. (Book 3, Chapter 6)

Love of others means service towards others.

Why should you mind serving others or being poor in the eyes of the world, as long as you do it for the love of Jesus Christ? (Book 1, Chapter 7)

CHAPTER 17

Meditation

While he dwelt on the earth ministering to others, Jesus was constantly thronged by people seeking His healing words or touch. But Jesus also took time to remove Himself from the crowds, and even His disciples, in order to pray and meditate. We, too, must meditate periodically on the things of God. In these passages below, Thomas recommended finding times of quiet and pondering to contemplate the goodness of God in our lives.

Make time to meditate on the things of God and not idle goings about.

Seek a convenient time to search your own conscience, meditating on the benefits of God. Restrain curiosity; read only those things that will move you to contrition rather than give you distraction. If you will withdraw from unnecessary talk and useless running about and listening to the latest gossip, you will find the time to occupy yourself in devout meditation. The greatest Saints avoided the company of worldly people as much as possible, for they preferred to be alone with God. (Book 1, Chapter 20)

Many are the admirers of contemplation, but few are willing to use the means needed for its attainment. It is a great hindrance to contemplation that we depend so much on outward signs and material things and practice little mortification. I do not know by what spirit we are led, nor what the aim is of those who are called spiritual persons, that we direct so much of our effort and solicitude toward transitory things, but seldom recollect our senses or give thought to the inward state of our own soul. The sad fact is that after a short period of meditation, we become involved in the external actions of everyday life without pausing to examine our conscience concerning all that we do. We pay no attention where our affections lie, nor do we have sorrow for our lack of pure intention and the sinfulness of our deeds. (Book 3, Chapter 31)

Humbly meditate on God's infinite goodness.

What better thought can I have for my soul's profit than to humble myself completely in Your presence, forever praising Your infinite goodness to me? (Book 4, Chapter 2)

CHAPTER 18

Nature of Man

One of the recurring sins of even some of the most devout Christians is to forget one's nature and assume an unshakeable goodness. Thomas reminded us that the nature of man is not God's nature. We are weak, prone to self-interest, shortsighted, and inclined to trust in flesh and not in God. Only when we realize that gap can we understand Jesus' role in closing it for us. This state is not eternal, according to Thomas. There is hope to put on the new man and make possible what our nature makes impossible.

Our natures are so far from God's.

Be full of grief and lament that you are still attached to the flesh and the world, so unmortified in your passions; so full of unsuppressed evil desires, so unguarded in your outward senses, so often engaged in useless imaginings; so readily drawn to things outside, so neglectful of those within.

Bewail the fact that you are so easily moved to laughter and frivolity, so slow to weep and repent; so inclined to relaxation and bodily comforts, so slothful in austerity and fervor of spirit; so eager for news and to see nice things, so reluctant to welcome humiliation and contempt; so craving for possessions, so stingy in giving and so obstinate in retaining. (Book 4, Chapter 7)

We are weak and easy to believe and speak evil of others.

It is not good to be taken in by every word or impulse that comes our way, but consider the thing prudently and thoughtfully in order not to offend God. Because we are frail we are always ready to believe the worst of people. Those who seek perfection realize that human nature is weak and prone to spread the evil word. (Book 1, Chapter 4)

The natural man does not understand the things of God that are understood by the spiritual man.

But a weak soul is yet incapable of detaching its heart perfectly from all things; nor can the carnal person understand the liberty of the spiritual person. (Book 3, Chapter 53)

The natural man is resentful when earthly desires are withdrawn.

When people desire anything to an excessive degree, they immediately lose their peace of soul. The proud and avaricious are always perturbed; while the humble and the poor in spirit live in peace and contentment. Those who are not mortified are easily overcome by small temptations. It is difficult for people to withdraw themselves from worldly desires when their spirits are still weak and inclined to the things of sense. While in this state their hearts are heavy when they try to detach themselves and they are quickly angered by those who oppose them. (Book 1, Chapter 6)

It is the nature of man to be deceived about worldly cares.

It is but a temptation that distresses you and a foolish fear that frightens you. This anxiety about future events brings you nothing but grief and more grief. *Today has troubles enough of its own* (Mt 6:34). It is a useless waste of time to worry or be elated about future events, which perhaps may never happen. But it is part of human nature to be deluded by the images of imagination, and the sign of a soul that is still weak that you so easily follow the suggestions of your enemy, the devil, who does not care whether his deceits are true or false, or whether he trips you up with the love of things present or fear of things to come. Therefore, *do not be distressed or fearful* (Jn 14:27). Have confidence in Me and trust in My mercy. When you think I am far away, I am often closest to you. When you think that almost all is lost, often a greater reward follows. (Book 3, Chapter 30)

It is in our nature to judge according to what we see. God does not do so.

Nature looks at the exterior of a person, but grace turns itself to the inward intention of the act. Nature is often mistaken, but grace trusts in God and is not deceived. (Book 3, Chapter 31)

It is the nature of man to be gluttonous.

Having to make use of food, drink, clothing and other necessities of the body is burdensome to a fervent soul. Grant me the grace to use such bodily necessities moderately and not to have an excessive desire for them. We are not permitted to dispense with them altogether, for nature must be sustained, but Your holy law forbids unnecessary luxuries to be sought for our mere pleasure; otherwise the flesh would rebel against the spirit. I beseech You, Lord, that Your hand govern and direct me in all these matters so that I avoid excess. (Book 3, Chapter 26)

God will help us conquer our wicked nature.

O Lord, my God, You have made me in Your own image and likeness; grant me this grace which You have shown me to be so great and so necessary for my salvation: to overcome my corrupt nature, which drags me down to sin and the loss of my soul. In my flesh I see the law of sin opposing the law of my mind, leading me into bondage; so that I incline more toward giving in to my sensual inclinations, nor am I able to resist these passions unless Your holy grace comes to my aid, infusing its fervor into my heart. (Book 3, Chapter 55)

The grace of God makes possible what seems impossible by our nature.

O Lord Jesus, make possible to me by grace what is impossible by nature. You know well how little I can bear and how easily I am upset by a little adversity. (Book 3, Chapter 19)

We must put on the new man of God.

You must still be tried here on earth and tested in many ways. Sometimes you will receive consolation, but never to your entire satisfaction. *Take courage and be strong* (Deut 31:7), whether in doing or in suffering things repugnant to nature. You must be changed into a new person, often doing what you would not do and leaving undone what you would like to do. Other people's interests will prosper, but your own will not succeed; others will be listened to, but people will pay no attention to what you say. Others will ask and shall receive, but your requests will be refused. Often people will say nice things about others, but never a good word about you. Others will be promoted to positions of trust, but you will be judged unfit.

Naturally, this kind of thing goes against the grain; but if you bear it in silence, you will advance considerably. For these—and many like things—are means by which the faithful servants of the Lord are tried, in order to determine how far they can deny and break their own will in all things. (Book 3, Chapter 49)

CHAPTER 19

Obedience

"If you love me, keep my commandments" (Jn 14:15). God does not ask for our half-hearted effort or, even worse, our mere lip service. Instead, He wants us to be obedient to His will. We must act, not just talk, in conformance to His will. Thomas admonished his readers to be willing to submit their own individual will to God's will. He also explained that we must understand that "following" is something we all must do throughout our lives. We will have others over us in various positions in life and therefore we must learn obedience. "No man safely commands, but he who loves to obey."

We must be obedient to God in all things.

Therefore, persons who keep themselves in subjection so that their sensuality obeys their reason, and their reason is obedient to Me in all things, are indeed, the true conquerors of themselves and the lords of the world. (Book 3, Chapter 53)

Be willing to submit to the will of others.

[T]hey who try to withdraw themselves from obedience withdraw themselves from grace. They who seek personal privileges lose those which are shared by all. If people do not freely and willingly submit themselves to a superior, it is a sign that their flesh is not completely under their control, but that it often rebels and complains. Therefore, if you want to subdue your lower nature, first learn to obey your superior. If the inner person is strong, the outward enemy is sooner overcome. There is no worse or more troublesome enemy to your soul than yourself, as long as your flesh is not under the control of your will. (Book 3, Chapter 13)

To be able to rule others we must be willing to be subject.

No one can be in the lead who is unwilling to remain in the background, and no one can govern with safety who does not know how to obey. (Book 1, Chapter 20)

CHAPTER 20

Patience

Often, life does not go the way we planned. Or we may be anxious about tomorrow and what it will bring. Or we may want something immediately and find ourselves frustrated that we cannot obtain it.

Thomas cautioned his readers about the tendency to be impatient. Patience is essential because we will not always have comforts or the absence of trials. Therefore, we must be patient to endure what God has given us. He will eventually reward us, but not necessarily on our timetable.

Patience is a necessity in a life of trouble.

O my Lord, God, I can see that patience is very necessary for me, for this life is full of many disturbing things. No matter how I may plan my life so as to have peace, life cannot be without struggle and sorrow. (Book 3, Chapter 12)

Do not doubt that God will reward.

If you are faithful and fervent in doing good, there is no doubt that God will be faithful and generous in His reward. (Book 1, Chapter 25)

Through patience, we can conquer with God's help.

It is only gradually—with patience and endurance and with God's grace—that you will overcome temptations sooner than by your own efforts and anxieties. (Book 1, Chapter 13)

Where is your faith? Stand firm and persevere. Have courage and wait patiently; comfort will come to you when you most need it. Wait for Me, wait; and I will come soon to help you. (Book 3, Chapter 30)

When consolation is withdrawn, do not be despondent, but humbly and patiently wait for the return of God; for He can give you back grace in fuller measure. (Book 2, Chapter 9)

To God, patience and humility in trials are better than ease.

I am more pleased, My child, when you are patient and humble under adversity than when you feel devout and consoled in prosperity. (Book 3, Chapter 57)

We should be calm in spirit to endure more difficult things.

Keep yourself calm and even prepare yourself to undergo greater suffering. All is not lost just because you find yourself often in trouble and grievously tempted. Remember, you are human and not God; you are flesh and blood and not an Angel. (Book 3, Chapter 57)

We must continue in patience when we feel bereft of God's help.

In whom, then, can I hope, or in what may I place my trust, but in the great and endless mercy of God? For whether I am in the company of good persons, devout brothers and sisters or faithful friends; or whether I have holy books, excellent treatises, or beautiful chants and hymns, what good will they all do me when grace is withdrawn and I am left with poverty? Patience is the best remedy in this state and the abandoning of self to the will of God. (Book 2, Chapter 9)

We can't always have spiritual comforts.

Why do you seek rest here when you are born to work? Dispose yourself to patience rather than to comfort and to carry the cross rather than to enjoyment. What temporal person would not gladly receive spiritual consolations if such a person could keep them always? Spiritual consolations far surpass all worldly enjoyments and bodily pleasures. For all worldly delights are either empty or unclean; but spiritual joys alone are delightful and honest, since they spring from virtue and are instilled by God into a pure soul. (Book 2, Chapter 10)

We must be patient with ourselves and others.

There will always be defects in ourselves or others which we cannot correct. These we must simply tolerate until God in His goodness sees fit to change things. After all, this may be the best possible way to prove our patience, without which our good qualities are not worth much. Nevertheless, you must pray earnestly that God in His mercy will help you to bear these impediments with patience. (Book 1, Chapter 16)

Christ suffered patiently; so must we.

My child, I came down from heaven to save you; I took upon Myself your miseries, not because I had to do so, but out of love. I wanted you to learn patience and to bear the trials of this life without complaint, as I have done for you. From the hour of My birth until My death upon the cross, I was never without sorrow or suffering. I endured the want of temporal things; many and frequent were the complaints I heard against Me; I humbly bore shame and insults. I received ingratitude for My benefits, blasphemies for My miracles, and rebukes for My true doctrine. (Book 3, Chapter 18)

When God's grace comes to any persons, they are made strong to do all things; and when it leaves them, they are poor and weak and left only as it were to the pain of bodily penances. But if this happens to you, do not be dejected nor despair, but resign yourself to the will of God, bearing whatever happens to you for the glory of Christ. For after winter follows summer, after night the day, and after the storm fair weather. (Book 2, Chapter 8)

A faithful servant of Christ bears adversity with patience.

Steel yourself, as a faithful servant of Christ, bravely to bear the cross of your Lord, Who out of love for you was nailed to the cross. Prepare yourself, then, to suffer all kinds of adversities and inconveniences in this wretched life; for you cannot avoid them no matter where you go, and they will find you no matter where you hide. So it is in life, and there is no avenue of escape but to keep yourself in patience. If you desire to be our Lord's dear friend and to share what is His, then you must drink heartily of His chalice. As for consolations, leave those to His will and He will arrange them as He sees best for you. (Book 2, Chapter 12)

We must wait in patience, therefore, having confidence in the mercy of God, until iniquity passes away and death is swallowed up in life eternal. (Book 1, Chapter 22)

JESUS WANTS US TO LIVE FOR HIM—"As the Father has loved Me, so have I loved you. Remain in My love. If you keep My commandments, you will remain in My love, just as I have kept My Father's commandments and remain in His love" (Jn 15:9f).

THE ALMIGHTY POWER OF JESUS—"[Jesus] entered the room where the [dead] child was. He took the child by the hand and said to her . . . 'Little girl, I say to you, arise!' And immediately the girl, a child of twelve, got up and began to walk around" (Mk 5:40ff).

If we are patient, we will receive the rewards of God

But think, My child, of the fruit of these hardships and what they will win for you; how soon they will end, when you will feel no more grief or pain, but the sweetest consolation of the Holy Spirit for your goodwill. In return for the weak will you freely surrender now, you will always have your own will in heaven; for there you will possess all good without fear of losing it.

There your will—always at one with Mine—will desire nothing for yourself alone apart from My desires. No one will resist you there, no one complain about you, and no one stand in your way. Every desirable good will be present simultaneously and all your powers of loving will be filled to the very brim.

There I will give you glory for the affronts you have endured, a robe of honor for your desolation, and a seat in My kingdom forever instead of the lowest place here. There your obedience will be rewarded, the toil of penance turned into joy, and humble submission receive a crown of glory. (Book 3, Chapter 49)

You must seek the grace of devotion with perseverance, waiting for it with patience and confidence, gratefully receiving it, humbly keeping it and carefully using it. The time and manner of this heavenly visit you must leave to God—until He wills to come to you. You should especially humble yourself when you feel little or no devotion; but do not be downcast or too upset about this. Often God is pleased to give in a single moment what He has withheld for a long time, sometimes bestowing at the end of prayer what He delayed giving when first you began to pray for it. (Book 4, Chapter 15)

God expects us to endure patiently..

What are you saying, My child? Stop complaining and consider My Passion and the sufferings of My Saints. *You have not yet resisted to the point of shedding your blood* (Heb 12:4).What you suffer is but little compared with those who have borne so much for Me, who have been strongly tempted, grievously afflicted and put to the test in so many ways. You ought to remind yourself of the intense sufferings that others have endured for Me, that you may bear your own little miseries more easily. If they do not seem so little to you, take care that you do not magnify them because of your impatience. However, whether they are little or great, always try to bear them patiently, willingly, and without complaint.

The better disposed you are to suffer them, the more wisely you act and the more merit you will have, because you have prepared yourself for it and are well disposed to accept it. Do not ever say: "I cannot endure this thing from such a person, nor should this be expected of me, for that person has done me a great wrong, accusing me of things I never thought of; but from someone else, I am willing to put up with what I think is fitting for me to suffer." This is a foolish thought, for you are forgetting the virtue of patience and by Whom its practice is rewarded, only considering the persons and the offenses done.

Therefore, they are not truly patient who will suffer only as much as they please and from whom they please. Persons who are really patient do not mind who causes their suffering— whether it be their superior, an equal, or someone of lower rank, or whether such a person is good and holy, or evil and unworthy. But whenever any adversity happens to them, whatever it is and from whomever it comes, or how often, they accept all gratefully as from the hand of God and consider it as a great benefit; for they well know that there is nothing we can suffer for God that goes without merit.

So, be ready to fight to win the victory. Without a conflict you cannot obtain the crown of patience. If you reject the suffering, you reject the crown also; but if you wish to be crowned, resist strongly and suffer patiently. There is no rest without labor, nor victory without battle. (Book 3, Chapter 19)

Better to endure joyfully, but at least we should do so patiently.

Resolve in your heart to do the best you can. Then when trials come your way, do not be downcast and do not go over and over them in your heart. If you cannot manage a smile, at least bear them with patience. Moreover, even though you feel indignant in your heart, control yourself and do not permit any inordinate word to escape your lips lest you scandalize the weak. In this way your indignation will soon calm down and grace will soon return to soothe your hurt feelings. I still live and am always ready to help and comfort you even more than before, if you will only fully trust Me and devoutly call upon Me. (Book 3, Chapter 57)

CHAPTER 21

Peace

Jesus said to His disciples: "Peace I leave with you, my peace I give unto you"(Jn 14:27). The peace Jesus is referring to is not peace between nations or merely the absence of conflict among people. Thomas identified traits of that peace.

Jesus' peace is not a peace that is dependent upon the approval of others. It does not come from busying ourselves with gossip or other people's business. His peace does not come from vanity, nor is it given to the wicked.

The Savior's peace is the result of humility. It is the product of relying on God and turning to Him for rest rather than to others or to material things. With God's peace, we can, in turn, become a peacemaker in the lives of others.

Peace does not come from acceptance by others.

Do not let your peace of mind depend on what people say about you. You are still what you are, no matter whether they put a good or bad interpretation on your actions. Where will you find true peace and true glory if not in Me? Certainly this is so. The person who neither aspires to please others nor fears to displease them will enjoy much peace; for all disquiet of heart and distraction of the senses come from disorderly affections and groundless fear. (Book 3, Chapter 28)

Peace comes from not worrying about the affairs of others.

We would indeed have peace if we would attend to our affairs. How can you remain in peace when you deliberately interfere in other people's business and seek worldly occupation with seldom a thought to interior recollection? The humble and the single-hearted are truly blessed and will have abundant peace. (Book 1, Chapter 11)

To have peace, it is necessary to cast off vain cares.

What a clear conscience we would have if we stopped running after passing pleasures and meddling in worldly affairs! What serenity we would have if we would do away with vain distractions and, thinking only of the things of God and our salvation, put all our confidence in Him. (Book 1, Chapter 20)

Those who turn their hearts to the Lord will find peace and rest.

Our Lord says: *"The kingdom of God is in your midst"* (Lk 17:21). The only way your soul will find rest is to turn to God with your whole heart and abandon this wretched world. Learn to despise exterior things and give your attention to the inner things; then you will see the kingdom of God come within you. The kingdom of God *means peace and joy in the Holy Spirit* (Rom 14:17), which is denied to evil people. Our Lord will visit the devout with His consolations, if they will make room for Him in the depths of their hearts. This is where He desires to be, and He will bring them many graces and much peace, and the sublime intimacy of His presence. (Book 2, Chapter 1)

Peace does not come to the wicked.

Evil persons are never really happy, nor do they feel peace within them; for *"there is no peace for the wicked, says the Lord"* (Isa 48:22). Even though the wicked may protest that peace is theirs and that no evil shall harm them, do not believe them. For God's wrath will suddenly overtake them, and all they have done will be brought to nothing and their plans destroyed. (Book 2, Chapter 6)

Peace does not come through dependence on others.

My child, if to satisfy yourself and to seek the society of any person you place all your contentment in that person, you will become entangled and lose your peace. On the other hand, if you have recourse only to Me, the living and everlasting Truth, you will not be overwhelmed if friends forsake you or you lose them by death. Whoever they may be, your friends must be loved for My sake, no matter how good they appear to you, or how dear they are to you in this life. No friendship can be profitable or lasting in this life, nor is it a true and pure love which does not have its source in Me. (Book 3, Chapter 42)

True peace is found only in heaven, not in the human person nor any other creature, but in God alone. (Book 3, Chapter 35)

Peace is with the humble and lowly in heart.

My child, I have said: *"Peace I leave with you, My peace I give to you. Not as the world gives do I give it to you"* (Jn 14:27). All human beings desire peace; but not all will do what is necessary to obtain it. My peace is found among the humble and gentle of heart; you will find your peace by being patient. If you will listen to Me and follow My words, you will enjoy great peace. (Book 3, Chapter 25)

When people desire anything to an excessive degree, they immediately lose their peace of soul. The proud and avaricious are always perturbed; while the humble and the poor in spirit live in peace and contentment. (Book 1, Chapter 6)

Peace comes from being proven through many trials.

O my Lord, God, I can see that patience is very necessary for me, for this life is full of many disturbing things. No matter how I may plan my life so as to have peace, life cannot be without struggle and sorrow.

My child, certainly this is true. It is not My will that you look for peace without temptations or difficulties; on the contrary, you must believe that you have found peace when you have been tried by tribulations and adversity. (Book 3, Chapter 12)

Peace comes from doing good.

If only you would think of the great interior peace you would have and how happy you would make others by doing good, you would be more eager to grow in virtue! (Book 1, Chapter 11)

Be at peace and then be a peacemaker.

You must first have peace in your own soul before you can make peace between other people. Peaceable people accomplish more good than learned people do. Those who are passionate often can turn good into evil and readily believe the worst. But those who are honest and peaceful turn all things to good and are suspicious of no one.

The discontented are easily troubled; they never know a quiet moment, nor will they leave others at rest. Many times they say the wrong thing and miss the chance of doing good. They are great for saying what others should do, but neglect their own duties. Begin by looking to your soul and then you will be better able to have zeal for your neighbor. (Book 2, Chapter 3)

CHAPTER 22

Prayer

For many, prayer is difficult because they consider it an admission of weakness and dependence. For others, prayer gets pushed aside in the rush of trivial daily tasks on which we place such great importance, but that actually pale in significance compared to prayer. Thomas explained the need to pray, why we pray, the times when we are in particular need of prayer, and what we receive from God when we pray. These passages are reminders that prayer is our personal communication with God, particularly in times of trial, and that the opportunity to commune with Him can be a sweet experience in our lives, if we will avail ourselves of it.

God is due our prayers of thanks and praise.

Accept my prayers, O Lord my God, and my desire to give You infinite praise and blessing, which are rightfully due to You because of Your surpassing greatness. All these I give You and desire to give You every day and every moment of time. With these dispositions and prayers, I invite and entreat all the heavenly spirits, as well as all the faithful, to join with me in thanking and praising You. (Book 4, Chapter 17)

We must learn to trust in God and not be slow to pray.

Come to Me when all is not well with you. What hinders you most of all from receiving heavenly consolation is your slowness in turning to Me in prayer. Before you pray earnestly to Me, you first seek other comforts, trying to find distraction in outward things. Hence it is that all these things are of little benefit to you until you realize that I alone am the One Who delivers those who trust in Me. (Book 3, Chapter 30)

We must fly to God to receive His counsel in our lives.

You, in turn, in all events must not let yourself be ruled by outward appearances, nor be guided by what you see or hear with carnal sentiments. But on every occasion enter, like Moses, into the Tabernacle to consult the Lord. Then you shall sometimes hear the divine answer and receive instruction for many things present and to come. For Moses always had recourse to the Tabernacle for resolving doubts and problems. He had recourse to prayer in the presence of dangers and the wickedness of people.

You must act similarly and, seeking shelter in the inmost depths of your heart, earnestly pray for divine help. Recall how Joshua and the children of Israel were misled by the Gibeonites because they did not first consult the Lord, but too easily believed those pleasing words and were taken in by false piety. (Book 3, Chapter 38)

We should pray when we feel far away from God.

If you find yourself dry, with no devotion, persevere in prayer, sigh and knock at My door; and do not stop until you receive some crumb or drop of this saving grace. (Book 4, Chapter 12)

It is important to concentrate on the Lord when we are praying so we can offer a "pure prayer."

In Your great mercy forgive me also all those times that I think of anything besides You in time of prayer; for I must confess—and You well know it, Lord—that I am usually very distracted. So often my thoughts are miles away from where my body stands or sits and these thoughts are mostly occupied with the things I love; the things I most readily think of are things that are pleasant to nature and the product of habit.

But You, O Eternal Truth, have plainly told us: *"Where your treasure is, there will your heart also be"* (Mt 6:21). So, if I love heaven, I love to think of heavenly things; but if I love the world, I rejoice at its prosperity and grieve over its adversity. If I love the spirit, I delight to think of spiritual things; but if I love the flesh, my imagination is occupied with the delights of the flesh. So whatever is uppermost in my affections, these I willingly listen to and speak of, and carry the thoughts of them often in my mind.

Blessed are those who abandon all things for love of You, O Lord, who overcome their nature and, through fervor of spirit, crucify the lusts of the flesh. Then with a serene conscience they may offer pure prayer to You, and at last become worthy to join the choirs of the holy Angels, having shut out all the internal and external things of this world. (Book 3, Chapter 48)

We should pray for forgiveness for the sins or offenses we have committed.

I offer You as well my prayers and this sacrifice of reconciliation especially for those who hurt me, offended me, abused me, or inflicted any injury upon me; and for all, too, whom I have at any time burdened, grieved, troubled or prevented from good—by word or deed, knowingly or unknowingly.

Be pleased to forgive us all our sins and mutual offenses. Drive from our hearts, O Lord, all suspicion, perversity, anger, dissension, and whatever else may wound charity or lessen brotherly love. Be merciful, O Lord, be merciful to those who implore Your mercy; give grace to those in need; make us all live in such a way as to be worthy to possess Your grace and life everlasting. Amen. (Book 4, Chapter 9)

CHAPTER 23

Pride

When Jesus' disciples argued among each other about who would be the greatest in Heaven, Jesus set a child in front of them and said: "Whoever humbles himself as this little child is the greatest in the kingdom of heaven"

FOLLOWING THE JUDGMENT OF JESUS—"Simon answered, 'Master, we worked hard throughout the night and caught nothing; but if You say so, I will let down the nets.' When they had done this, they caught . . . a great number of fish" (Lk 5:5ff).

RECOURSE TO JESUS IN TRIALS—"The blind receive their sight, the lame walk, those who have leprosy are cleansed, the deaf hear, the dead are raised to life, the poor have the good news proclaimed to them" (Lk 7:22).

(Mt 18:4). Greatness does not come from pride; it comes from humility. Thomas understood that pride separates us from God, while humility brings the Spirit of God into our lives. In these passages, he provides practical ways to avoid the sin of pride in order to remain humble before God.

Be not high-minded.

No matter how much you know, realize how much there is that you do not know. Do not be afraid to acknowledge your own ignorance. Why have an exalted opinion of yourself when you know there are many, even in your own field, whose knowledge surpasses yours? If you want to learn anything worthwhile, seek rather to be unknown and to be thought of as nothing. (Book 1, Chapter 2)

Avoid boasting about God's gifts.

Do not boast of riches if you have them, or of your important friends; but glory in God only, from Whom all good things come and Who, being the highest good, desires to give us Himself. Do not boast of beauty of body, which is soon disfigured by illness or age. Do not be proud of any talents or skills you possess, for in this way you displease God from Whom you have received them. (Book 1, Chapter 7)

Don't be proud of good works.

Do not consider yourself better than others, for you may be worse in God's sight. Do not be proud of your good works, for often what pleases us displeases God, Whose judgments differ from the judgment of humans. Whatever goodness or virtue is in you, believe that your neighbor has better qualities; in this way you will preserve humility. It will not hurt you to consider yourself worse than others, even if this is not really so; but it will hurt greatly if you prefer yourself above another, although that person might be a great sinner. A humble person is a peaceful person; but the hearts of the proud are full of envy and resentment. (Book 1, Chapter 7)

Avoid overconfidence.

Often those who have enjoyed the esteem of others are in grave danger because they are overconfident. It is a good thing that many of us are not free of temptations, for these make us watchful so that we do not become proud and rely upon worldly consolation. (Book 1, Chapter 20)

To avoid pride, renounce self-love.

It is hard to find anyone so spiritual who is willing to be stripped of all things. Where will you find a person truly poor in spirit and free from all attachment to creatures? Such a one is a *rare treasure brought from distant shores* (Prov 31:14). If we were to give up all our possessions, it is still nothing; if we did severe penance, it is but little; if we acquired all knowledge, still are we far from virtue. Even if we had great virtue and fervent devotion, we would be lacking that one thing necessary above all else.

And what is that one thing? That leaving all things behind, we should leave self, renouncing our self completely and keeping nothing of self-love. And then when we have done all things that we know we ought to do, let us think that we have done nothing.

We should not regard as great that which may be considered so by others, but rather let us in truth look upon ourselves as worthless servants. As our Lord, the Truth, has said: *"When you have done all you were ordered to do, say, 'We are unprofitable servants'"* (Lk 17:10). Then will we be truly poor in spirit and able to say with the Prophet: *"I am alone and afflicted"* (Ps 25:16). Yet there is no one richer or more powerful, no one more free than we are if we know how to renounce ourselves and all things, putting ourselves in the lowest place. (Book 2, Chapter 11)

To overcome pride, we should have a humble opinion of ourselves.

Oh, what a lowly and humble opinion I ought to have of myself, and how little I ought to regard whatever good I may seem to have! (Book 3, Chapter 14)

CHAPTER 24

Prudence

All of us seek to avoid mistakes and bypass the pitfalls of life. Thomas urged prudence and linked the attainment of that virtue to our willingness to be a disciple of Christ. Those who seek to follow Christ can learn to be prudent and confident in God.

Grace makes us humble and prudent.

I gladly accept that grace which makes me more humble and prudent and more ready to deny myself. (Book 2, Chapter 10)

We must consider things prudently to avoid offending God.

It is not good to be taken in by every word or impulse that comes our way, but consider the thing prudently and thoughtfully in order not to offend God. (Book 1, Chapter 4)

If we have confidence in God, we are more likely to act carefully and prudently.

Who is there who can behave so carefully and prudently in all things as not to be sometimes mistaken or perplexed? Certainly very few. But those who have complete confidence in You, O Lord—seeking You in the simplicity of their hearts—do not slip away from You so easily. (Book 3, Chapter 45)

Don't be taken in by others' flattery.

Grant me the prudence to avoid all flatterers. (Book 3, Chapter 27)

Prudence means understanding our limits.

Some imprudent people, through an indiscreet desire to have the grace of devotion, have damaged themselves, for they wished to do more than they were able. Not taking into account the limit of their gift or their own weakness, they chose to follow their inclinations rather than good judgment; and because they presumed to undertake more than was pleasing to God, they soon lost the grace they already had. They were left poor and abandoned, for they thought they had built a nest in heaven for themselves. In this way they were taught not to rely on their own strength, but humbly to trust in God and His goodness. (Book 3, Chapter 7)

CHAPTER 25

Purity

Jesus told the scribes and Pharisees that they must cleanse the inside of the cup and not just the outside of it (Mt 23:25). He meant that they overemphasized the external things— those things that could be seen and counted by others—and did not concern themselves with what was internal—that which could be seen only by God. Thomas discussed why we need to be pure of heart and not just outwardly religious. He offered advice on what purity of heart does for us and how we can be pure before God.

What the pure in heart are like.

A pure, simple and stable heart is not bogged down by a multitude of tasks because it does all for the honor of God, and since it is not self-seeking, it is not eager to follow its own will. (Book 1, Chapter 3)

How purity of heart changes us.

If there is any true joy in this world, only the person with a clean conscience possesses it. And wherever there is misery and affliction, the evil conscience experiences it best. Iron cast into the fire loses its rust and becomes clean and bright; and those who make God the center of their lives are cleansed of slothfulness and are changed into new persons. The moment you begin to grow lukewarm, everything is a big effort and you willingly receive distractions from without. But as soon as you begin to conquer yourself and walk uprightly in the way of God, then the effort expended seems little which before you thought was insurmountable. (Book 2, Chapter 4)

Purity means being free from inordinate affection and seeing others as a reflection of the goodness of God.

We are lifted up above earthly things by two wings: simplicity and purity. Simplicity regulates the intentions and purity the affections. Simplicity looks to God and purity finds Him and savors Him. No good work will hinder you if your heart is free from inordinate affections; on the contrary, you will grow in the way of perfection. If your main object is the will of God and the good of your neighbor, you will have great interior freedom. If your heart is straight with God, then every creature will be a mirror of life and a book of heavenly teaching. There is no creature so insignificant and small which does not reflect the goodness of God. (Book 2, Chapter 4)

A pure heart understands correctly.

If you had a heart that was good and pure you would see all things clearly and understand them well. A clean heart penetrates both heaven and hell. As people are inwardly, so do they judge outward things. (Book 2, Chapter 4)

CHAPTER 26

Self-esteem

What we think of ourselves influences what we think of God and others. But where that self-esteem comes from is critical to our attitudes and behavior towards God and others. Thomas à Kempis reminded his readers that self-esteem must come from God and not from others. We can easily be deceived by others dictating what we should think of ourselves. The honors bestowed by others are no substitute for God's evaluation of who we are. We must be humble in our self-assessment rather than elevate ourselves. We must be satisfied with less and be humble rather than to have much and become proud.

We will fall if we rely on the esteem of others; instead we should put our hope in God.

Often those who have enjoyed the esteem of others are in grave danger because they are overconfident. It is a good thing that many of us are not free of temptations, for these make us watchful so that we do not become proud and rely upon worldly consolation. What a clear conscience we would have if we stopped running after passing pleasures and meddling in worldly affairs! What serenity we would have if we would do away with vain distractions and, thinking only of the things of God and our salvation, put all our confidence in Him. (Book 1, Chapter 20)

It is better to have less than to be proud because we have more.

Seldom are the wise in their own estimation humble enough to allow others to guide them. Therefore, it is better to have a little learning with humility than great learning with self-complacency. It is better to have a little learning with grace than much learning which fills you with pride. (Book 3, Chapter 7)

We don't realize our own inward blindness and instead think too highly of ourselves.

We cannot count on ourselves much, for often through lack of grace and understanding our judgment is a limited one and we soon lose what we have through our own neglect. Often we are unaware of our own interior blindness. Many times we do evil and, what is far worse, we justify it.

Sometimes our passions rule us and we mistake it for zeal. We are critical of the small defects in our neighbors, but overlook the serious faults in ourselves. We are quick to complain of what we put up with from others, with never a thought of what others suffer from us. If we would see ourselves as we really are, we would not find cause to judge others severely. (Book 2, Chapter 5)

We should count ourselves less rather than more; we find ourselves when we love God rather than center our love on ourselves.

I will speak to You, Lord Jesus, *I who am but dust and ashes* (Gen 18:27). If I think myself any better, You stand opposed to me, and what is more, my own sins bear witness against me. This evidence I cannot deny.

But if I humble myself, admit my insignificance, rid myself of all self-esteem, and regard myself as the mere dust that I am, then Your grace will come to me and the light of Your understanding enter into my heart; so that, through perfect knowledge of my wretchedness, all self-esteem will be lost in the depth of my own nothingness. There You show me what I truly am, what I have been, and what I have become; for I am nothing and I did not know it. Left to myself, I realize then that I am nothing and that all is weakness and imperfection. But the moment You look upon me, I soon become strong and am filled with new joy. How wonderful it is that I am so quickly lifted up and so lovingly supported by You, I who of myself tend downward to earthly things.

Lord, Your love is the cause of this, which goes before me and helps me in all my necessities; it protects me from those grave dangers to which I am most prone to succumb. I have lost You and myself, too, by my disordered self-love; by seeking You again, I found both You and myself. From now on, therefore, I will make myself completely insignificant and more earnestly seek You; for You, Lord Jesus, deal with me far above what I deserve—indeed far above all that I dare to ask or hope for.

Blessed are You, O Lord, in all Your works, for though I am unworthy of any good, You continually surround me with Your kindness, which is extended even to those who are ungrateful to You or have turned away from You. Lord, please turn us back to You again so that we may become grateful, humble and devout; for You are our help, our salvation and the strength of our body and soul. (Book 3, Chapter 8)

CHAPTER 27

Self-Mastery

Control over self and even the denial of things that we want is the only way to follow Christ. Thomas explained the importance of being the master over our own desires and passions in order to serve Christ. Without the mastery we would be slaves to carnal desires, but with it we gain happiness with Christ.

We must strive for self-mastery.

My child, strive diligently for perfect interior freedom and self-mastery in every place, in every action and occupation, so that you be not the slave of anything, but that all things be under your control. You must be lord and ruler over your actions, never a bondsman or a mercenary.

You must be a free person—similar to a righteous Hebrew—one who is transferred to the rank and the liberty of the children of God. Children of God stand above present things; they contemplate those that are eternal. They look upon transient things with the left eye; with the right eye they look at heavenly things. They do not allow temporal things to attract them, nor do they cling to them; instead they make those earthly things serve the end and purpose for which God made and ordained them. (Book 3, Chapter 38)

To be Christ's disciple, we must practice self-denial.

But if you wish to enter into life, keep the commandments (Mt 19:17); if you want to know the truth, believe Me. *If you wish to be perfect, go, sell your possessions* (Mt 19:21). If you want to be My disciple, deny yourself. (Book 3, Chapter 56)

We can die happy if we deny self to serve God.

How happy and wise are those who try now to become what they would want to be at the hour of death. A perfect contempt of the world, an ardent desire to progress in virtue, a love of discipline, a prompt obedience, a denial of self and a patient bearing of all adversities for the love of Christ will give you great confidence of dying happily. (Book 1, Chapter 23)

CHAPTER 28

Serving God

As one who sought to serve God, Thomas considered what service to God really meant and why and how it should be conducted. These passages are reminders of God's gifts to those in His service. Thomas understood that we are not really serving God. Even in our "service" God is doing much more to serve us.

We should serve God and others, but for the right reasons.

Those who love God much do much, and those do a deed well who perform it for the common good and not to please themselves. Often what appears to be charity is really done for carnal motives—self-love, the hope of a reward or some personal advantage seldom being absent. (Book 1, Chapter 15)

Oh how powerful is the pure love of Jesus, when not mixed with self-interest or self-love! Are not they to be called hirelings who always look for comforts? And they who think only of their own advantage, do they not show themselves to be lovers of self rather than of Christ? Where will a person be found ready to serve God without looking for a reward? (Book 2, Chapter 11)

God will reward us for being in His service.

Your labor will last but a short time and then you will receive everlasting rest and peace. If you are faithful and fervent in doing good, there is no doubt that God will be faithful and generous in His reward. Have a firm hope that you will attain the victory; but do not presume on this, for then there is danger of your becoming careless and proud. (Book 1, Chapter 25)

While in God's service, don't worry about what will happen in the future but just do the will of God now.

Once there was a person who was anxious whether or not he was in the state of grace; one day in his sadness, he fell to his knees before an altar in the church, praying: "Oh, if only I knew whether I would persevere to the end of my life!"

Suddenly he heard a voice within him, answering: "What would you do if you did know? Do now what you would do then and you will be secure." Immediately he was comforted and commended himself entirely to God's will and all his doubts ceased. After that, he never speculated as to what would become of him. Instead he applied himself to know what was the will of God for him and how he might begin and end all his good works to the honor and glory of God. (Book 1, Chapter 25)

Use time wisely; carry out service with diligence.

Always remember your end and that time lost can never be regained. Without applying yourself diligently, you will never acquire virtue. The moment you begin to be lukewarm, your trouble begins.

But, if you give yourself wholeheartedly to fervor, you will experience great help from God and you will find the pursuit of virtue less burdensome than you did at first. Those who are fervent and loving will always be ready to do God's will. It is harder to resist vices and passions than to toil and sweat in bodily labors. If you do not shun little faults, you will gradually fall into greater ones. If you spent the day well, you will be happy when night comes.

Watch yourself, stir yourself up, warm yourself; whatever your obligation to others, do not neglect your own soul. The more restraints you put on yourself, the more spiritual progress you will make and the greater your attachment to the will of God. (Book 1, Chapter 25)

It is God who is really serving us rather than us Him.

You know, O Lord, all that I have is Yours, even those things with which I serve You. But in Your goodness, it is rather You Who serve me than I You. For the heavens and the earth, which You have created for our use, are ready day by day to carry out Your commands. You have also appointed Your Angels to serve our needs. And as if this were not enough, You stoop to serve us Yourself, promising to give Yourself to us. (Book 3, Chapter 10)

We are poor servants.

And now what shall I give You in return for these innumerable blessings? O my God, if only I

JESUS THE BREAD OF LIFE—"Whoever eats My Flesh and drinks My Blood dwells in Me, and I dwell in him. . . . This is the Bread that came down from heaven. . . . the one who eats this Bread will live forever" (Jn 6:56ff).

PRUDENCE IN WORLDLY AFFAIRS—"[Jesus] asked them, 'Whose image is this, and whose inscription?' They replied and said to Him, 'Caesar's.' Jesus said to them, 'Give to Caesar what is due to Caesar, and to God what is due to God' " (Mk 12:16f).

could serve You all the days of my life—or even for one day be able to serve You faithfully; for You are worthy of all honor, service and praise forever. You are my Lord and my God, and I am Your poorest servant, bound to serve You with all my strength and never to grow weary of praising You. This is my desire, this I implore You: that I may always praise You and that You will supply whatever is wanting to me. (Book 3, Chapter 10)

It is a great honor to be in the service of God and our reward is God's grace.

It is a great honor to serve You, and to despise all things for love of You. Those who freely give themselves to Your holy service will receive great grace. (Book 3, Chapter 10)

CHAPTER 29

Simplicity

Mysteries and complexities intrigue us. But that is not where God is; nor is it where He wants us to be. Thomas stressed the importance of staying with the humble and simple rather than seeking after "hidden and dark things" that divert us from the Gospel.

We must concentrate on what is simple and not on hidden and dark things.

What good will it do us to learn many things, the knowledge of which will not help us on judgment day, nor hurt us if we do not know them? It is foolish not to learn those things which are necessary for us and to waste our time on those that merely satisfy our curiosity and hurt us in the end. For if we do so, we have eyes but cannot see. (Book 1, Chapter 3)

That simplicity is truly blessed which departs from ways of dispute and follows the plain and sure path of God's commandments. Many have lost their devotion while searching into mysteries too deep for them to understand. Only faith and a good life are required of you, not a lofty intellect nor a probing into the deep mysteries of God.

If you cannot understand or grasp those things which are beneath you, how can you comprehend those that are above you? Submit yourself humbly to God, and submit your senses to faith, and the light of knowledge will be given to you for your spiritual well-being, according to the measure of God. (Book 4, Chapter 18)

Walk in the simplicity of heart.

My child, *walk before Me in truth* (1 Ki 2:4) and simplicity of heart—without pretense. Those who so walk will be shielded from the attacks of the evil one; and Truth shall free them from deceivers and the detractions of evil people. If Truth makes you free, you will be free indeed and the vain words of human beings will not bother you. (Book 3, Chapter 4)

CHAPTER 30

Temptation

The New Testament related that Jesus was tempted by Satan, but did not succumb. So, too, we are tempted in this life. But, with God's help, we can overcome temptation and cast Satan away from us. Thomas wrote that temptation should not be a surprise—it is a constant throughout our lives. Therefore, we must constantly be aware of it. He described where temptation comes from—forces external to us—and how temptation can be useful to us in purification and instruction. He also provided a warning; Satan will repeatedly tempt us and we must wear spiritual armor to protect ourselves.

Also, if we succumb to temptation, it is not the end. There is repentance and forgiveness. Then, we must go forward with renewed vigor.

We must pass through "fire and water."

When you are troubled, that is the best time for you to merit. Yes, you must pass through fire and water before you come to the place of refreshment. Unless you gain full control of yourself, you will never overcome sin, and life will always be a burden because of the frailty of our nature. (Book 1, Chapter 22)

We will always be tempted and tried.

We will never be free of trials and temptations as long as our earthly life lasts. For Job has said: *"Is not the life of human beings on earth a drudgery?"*

(Job 7:1). Therefore, we should always be on our guard against temptations, always praying that our enemy, the devil, *who never sleeps but constantly looks for someone to devour* (1 Pet 5:8), will not catch us off guard. No one in this world is so perfect or holy as not to have temptations sometimes. We can never be entirely free of them. (Book 1, Chapter 13)

Temptation is useful as a means for purification and instruction.

Sometimes these temptations can be very severe and troublesome, but if we resist them, they will be very useful to us; for by experiencing them we are humbled, cleansed and instructed. (Book 1, Chapter 13)

All are subject to temptation, but heavenly comfort follows temptation.

I have never known anyone so religious and devout who has not sometimes had a withdrawal of grace or felt a diminishing of fervor. Never was a Saint so greatly enraptured or enlightened as not to be tempted at some time. For no persons are worthy of high contemplation unless they have suffered some tribulation for God. Temptation going before is often a sign that consolation will follow. For to those who have been proved by temptation heavenly consolation is promised. *"To those who are victorious, I will give the right to eat from the tree of life"* (Rev 2:7). (Book 2, Chapter 9)

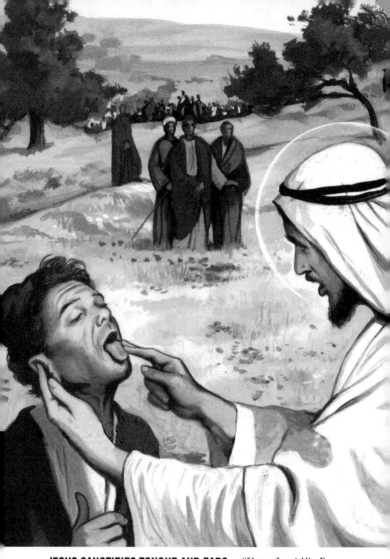

JESUS SANCTIFIES TONGUE AND EARS—"[Jesus] put His fingers into the man's ears and, spitting, touched his tongue.... He sighed and said to him, *'Ephphatha!'* which means, 'Be opened!' At once, the man's ears were opened . . . and he spoke properly" (Mk 7:33ff).

JESUS CAN OVERCOME ALL TRIALS—"Jesus responded, 'Amen, amen, I say to you, before Abraham was, I AM!' On hearing this, they picked up stones to throw at Him, but Jesus hid Himself and left the temple" (Jn 8:58f).

*We should not procrastinate in our deter-
mination to change and reform.*

O my brother or sister, do not lose your desire
for spiritual progress while time and opportunity
still await you! Why do you delay any longer? Get
up; now is the time to begin! Say to yourself:
"Now is the time for good works, now is the time
to fight, now is the time to make reparation for the
sins of the past." (Book 1, Chapter 22)

When temptation comes, cast Satan away.

Turn his malice against him, saying to him: Be-
gone, Satan, you wicked spirit, and be ashamed, for
you are foul to suggest such things to me. Depart
from me, you father of lies. You shall have no hold
upon me; for Jesus Christ, my Savior, is with me as
my valiant defender, and you shall be put to flight
in utter confusion. I would rather die in torment
than give in to you. Be silent and cease your malice,
for I will not listen to you no matter how much you
tempt me. *The Lord is my light and my salvation;
whom should I fear? Even if an army encamps against
me, my heart will not succumb to fear. You are my help
and my deliverer* (Pss 27:1, 3; 40:18).

Fight on like a good soldier; and if sometimes
through weakness you fall, get up again and with
greater strength than before, trust in My abundant
grace. But be on your guard against self-complacency and pride; for it is through these that many
are led into error, and sometimes into an almost
incurable blindness of soul. (Book 3, Chapter 6)

We are all tempted differently.

Temptations differ with different people: some are greatly tempted in the first stages of turning to God; some have it in their later days; while still others have it all their lives, and there are also those who are only lightly tempted. But it is all part of God's plan for us,Whose wisdom and justice knows each person's state and orders all things rightly for the salvation of His elect. (Book 1, Chapter 13)

Temptations come from outward things; the disciple of Christ walks from within.

They are wise who observe things as they are and not by what is said about them, or by the value put on them; for they are taught by God and not by humans. Those who can raise their minds to God, with little regard to outward things, do not need to look for place or time to pray or to do good deeds.

For interior persons, not being wholly occupied with the things of sense, can easily fix their minds on God. Their exterior work is no obstacle to them, nor is any necessary employment; they will apply themselves to each in turn and refer all to the will of God. If your soul is well disposed and disciplined, you will not be surprised or disturbed by the perverse conduct of others.You will be hindered and distracted to the extent that you are taken up with worldly matters.

If you were well purified from worldly attachments, whatever happened would turn to your spiritual profit and to an increase of grace and virtue in your soul. But because of your excess love of earthly things, many things displease and annoy you. (Book 2, Chapter 1)

The strong lover of God stands fast in temptations and disbelieves the devil's persuasions.

Because with a little adversity you leave off what you have begun and eagerly seek outward consolation. Valiant lovers of God stand firm in time of temptation and pay no attention to the deceitful suggestions of their enemy, the devil. When all goes well with them, I please them; and so do I please them when things go wrong. (Book 3, Chapter 6)

Satan is constantly seeking to tempt and entrap us.

It is essential for our true spiritual progress that we deny ourselves. And those who have renounced themselves obtain great liberty and enjoy great safety. The old enemy, however, who wars against everything that is good, does not fail to tempt us. Day and night he uses dangerous tricks to trap the unwary. Hence we are told: *Stay awake and pray that you may not enter into temptation* (Mt 26:41). (Book 3, Chapter 39)

Our spiritual armor against temptation is necessary as long as we live.

My child, you are never secure in this life. As long as you live you will always need spiritual weapons. You are in the midst of enemies, who may attack from the right hand or the left. If you do not make use of the shield of patience on all occasions, it is certain you will be wounded before long.

Moreover, if you do not fix your heart on Me, with the sincere will to endure all things for My sake, you will be unable to stand up under the heat of battle and will fail to win the palm I reserve for My Saints. Therefore, you must bear all courageously, using a strong hand against all that stands in your way. The person who overcomes is fed with the Bread from heaven, but to the coward is left much misery. (Book 3, Chapter 35)

We need God's help to overcome temptation.

I labor, indeed, in the sweat of my brow; I am tormented by a sorrowful heart, burdened by my sins, troubled with temptations, and caught up in and oppressed by many evil passions, but there is no one to help me. For who can deliver me and save me, and to whom can I commit myself and all that is mine, except You, Lord God, my Savior? (Book 4, Chapter 4)

Many try to fly away from temptations only to fall more deeply into them; for you cannot win a battle by mere flight. It is only by patience and humility that you will be strengthened against the enemy.

JESUS, LORD OF NATURE—"Then [Jesus] said, 'Young man, I say to you, arise!' The dead man sat up and began to speak, and Jesus gave him to his mother" (Lk 7:14f).

JESUS ENTRUSTS HIMSELF INTO THE FATHER'S HANDS—"It was now about noon, and darkness came over the whole land. . . . Jesus cried out, 'Father, into Your hands I commend My spirit.' And with these words He breathed His last" (Lk 23:44, 46).

Those who only shun them outwardly and do not pull them out by the roots will make no progress; for temptations will soon return to harass them and they will be in a worse state. It is only gradually—with patience and endurance and with God's grace—that you will overcome temptations sooner than by your own efforts and anxieties. (Book 1, Chapter 13)

We must be patient in times of temptation and if we fall in weakness, get up again and again and continue to trust in God.

What shall I say now, Lord, in the midst of my distress? May Your will be done, for I well deserve to be afflicted and oppressed. I must bear it—and with patience—until the storm has passed and things grow better. (Book 3, Chapter 29)

Just because we receive spiritual comfort from God does not mean there will not be more temptation to follow.

However, when God sends you spiritual comfort, accept it gladly and thank Him for it, but fully realize that it is God's mercy that sends it and not any deserving of yours. Do not be proud, presumptuous or overjoyed; rather let this gift humble you and be wary and fearful in all you do; for surely that time will pass away and be followed by temptation. (Book 2, Chapter 9)

Be always prepared for temptation.

God gives consolation to make us stronger in time of adversity. Then temptations follow to prevent us from becoming proud, thinking we are worthy of such a favor. The devil never sleeps, neither is the flesh yet dead; therefore you must always be prepared to do battle, for you are surrounded by enemies that never rest. (Book 2, Chapter 9)

To avoid temptation, be more displeased with sin than with the loss of material things.

Fear nothing so much, blame and avoid nothing so much as your sins and vices, which ought to distress you more than the loss of all worldly possessions. (Book 3, Chapter 4)

This is how temptation is: first we have a thought, followed by strong imaginings, then the pleasure and evil emotions, and finally consent. This is how the enemy gains full admittance, because he was not resisted at the outset. The slower we are to resist, the weaker we daily become and the stronger the enemy is against us. (Book 1, Chapter 13)

CHAPTER 31

Wisdom

"The fear of the Lord is the beginning of wisdom" (Prov 9:10). The wisdom God seeks for us is not to be street-savvy or shrewd. Rather it is the wisdom of one who steadfastly follows Christ. Thomas understood that the wisdom that matters eternally is the wisdom that comes from God. In these passages, he explains who is wise, what constitutes wisdom, and how wisdom is different from secular knowledge.

Our wisdom comes from God.

There can be no hope of holiness, O Lord, if You withdraw Your merciful hand. No wisdom can benefit us, if You cease to rule. (Book 3, Chapter 14)

The wise man is the one who is despised for Christ.

Then those will appear to have been wise in this world who contented themselves to be taken for fools and despised for the sake of Christ. They will be glad that they suffered tribulation patiently in this world, for all iniquity shall stop its mouth.

Every devout person shall be joyful, while the irreligious will be sad. The flesh that was chastised shall exult more than if it had been pampered with luxuries. The shabby garment shall shine and the fine clothing look like rags. The poor dwelling shall be more celebrated than the gilded palace, constant patience shall help more than all worldly power, and simple obedience shall be rated higher than all worldly cunning. (Book 1, Chapter 24)

The signs of wisdom.

It is wise, therefore, to act slowly, not to trust entirely our own opinions, or to accept every tale and quickly pass it along to the next one. Seek advice from a wise person of good conscience and be instructed by that person rather than follow your own way. (Book 1, Chapter 4)

Beginners and those inexperienced in the way of the Lord may easily fall into error and be deceived unless they seek the counsel of the wise. (Book 3, Chapter 7)

My child, hear My words and follow them; for they are most sweet and far exceed the learning and wisdom of the philosophers and all the wise of the world. (Book 3, Chapter 29)

True heavenly wisdom is so cheaply regarded by humans as to be almost forgotten; for this heavenly wisdom goes against nature because it does not hold a high opinion of self, nor does it seek worldly renown. (Book 3, Chapter 32)

Help me to regard all things in this world as they are—passing and short-lived—realizing that I, too, will pass away with them. Nothing under the sun is lasting, but *all is vanity and a chase after wind* (Eccl 1:14). It is a wise person who understands this. (Book 3, Chapter 27)

God's wisdom is greater than secular knowledge.

There is a vast difference between the wisdom of an enlightened and devout soul and the knowledge of a learned and studious scholar. The knowledge which is poured into the soul by the influence of God's grace is far nobler than that which is acquired by human labor and study. (Book 3, Chapter 31)

Cast aside worldly wisdom, which seeks to please the world and self. (Book 3, Chapter 32)

My child, hear My words and follow them; for they are most sweet and far exceed the learning and wisdom of the philosophers and all the wise of the world. (Book 3, Chapter 3)

The wise are steadfast in their devotion to Christ.

My child, do not trust your present affections, for they quickly change from one to another. As long as you live, your moods will change, even though you do not will it. Sometimes you are happy, at other times sad; now you are at peace, then you are upset; at one time devout, at another spiritually dry; sometimes full of vigor, at other times sluggish; one day elated, the next day gloomy.

But those who are wise and have been well instructed in the spiritual life rise above these changing moods, ignoring their inner feelings and on what side the wind of instability blows, so long as the direction of their souls advances toward their desired goal. Thus they can remain stable and unshaken through many changing events, always directing their intention toward Me. (Book 3, Chapter 33)

To be wise, we must set our goal on heaven.

The height of wisdom is to set your goal on heaven by despising the world. (Book 1, Chapter 1)

OTHER OUTSTANDING CATHOLIC BOOKS

EVERY DAY IS A GIFT—Introduction by Rev. Frederick Schroeder. Short, popular meditations for every day, featuring a text from Sacred Scripture, a timeless quotation from the writings of a Saint, and a meaningful prayer. Printed in two colors. **No. 195**

ST. JOSEPH SUNDAY MISSAL—The complete Masses for Sundays, Holydays, and the Sacred Paschal Triduum. Includes the Readings for the 3-year Cycle (A, B, and C) and Mass texts in accord with *The Roman Missal,* Third Edition. **No. 820**

CHRISTIAN PRAYER—The official one-volume edition of the internationally acclaimed *Liturgy of the Hours.* This version contains the complete texts of Morning and Evening Prayer for the entire year. The large type is ideal for those with difficulty in reading. **No. 406**

CATHOLIC BOOK OF PRAYERS—GIANT TYPE EDITION. Rev. Maurus FitzGerald, O.F.M. Today's most popular general prayer book. Contains many favorite prayers—for every day, to the Blessed Trinity, to Mary, and to the Saints, as well as a summary of our Faith. **No. 910**

THE IMITATION OF CHRIST—GIANT TYPE EDITION. This treasured book has brought peace to readers for many ages by showing how to follow the life of Christ to which all are called. **No. 322**

THE IMITATION OF CHRIST (Abridged Edition)—Adapted by Sr. Halcon J. Fisk. This classic work on the spiritual life is adapted for contemporary readers. Contains the essence of Thomas à Kempis's masterpiece in digestible form. **No. 362**

FAVORITE PRAYERS FROM THE IMITATION OF CHRIST—A book of prayers taken from the classic work of Thomas à Kempis. All the prayers are given in large type and sense lines for easier reading and understanding. Printed in two colors. 192 pages. **No. 927**

INTRODUCTION TO A DEVOUT LIFE—Adapted by Sr. Halcon J. Fisk. St. Francis de Sales, known as the apostle of love, reached out to everyone through this small book, showing that devotion is available to everyone in every walk of life and occupation. **No. 163**

THE IMITATION OF MARY—By Rev. Alexander de Rouville, S.J. Modern version of the companion volume to *The Imitation of Christ.* The author follows the Blessed Virgin through the different mysteries and circumstances of her life. Contains full-color inserts. **No. 330**

TREASURY OF NOVENAS—By Rev. Lawrence G. Lovasik, S.V.D. More than forty popular Novenas carefully arranged for private prayer in accord with the Liturgical Year on the Feasts of Jesus, Mary, and favorite Saints. With full-color inserts and Dura-Lux cover. **No. 345**

ISBN 978-1-941243-39-8